Helen Trinca is editor of *AFR BOSS*, the leadership and management magazine published by *The Australian Financial Review*. She has worked in senior reporting and editing roles in Australian journalism. Her previous positions include London correspondent and deputy editor at *The Australian*. As workplace writer at *The Sydney Morning Herald* she co-authored (with Anne Davies) the definitive history of one of the nation's biggest industrial disputes, the 1998 docks battle. The book, *Waterfront: The Battle that Changed Australia*, was published in 2000 by Random House.

Catherine Fox is deputy editor of *AFR BOSS* magazine and writes a weekly column, 'Workspace', for *The Australian Financial Review*. She joined the *AFR* in 1989 and has held a variety of positions, including marketing and Smart Money editor, 'Corporate Woman' columnist and court reporter (winning the NSW Law Society's journalism award). Before joining the *AFR* she worked in financial marketing and consulting in Sydney and London. Catherine has worked for a range of large and small organisations, including two of Australia's largest banks, a university and an advertising agency. As the mother of three daughters, she has also tested most working combinations: as a full-time carer or employee, a part-time worker or student, and a freelancer.

better than
SEX

How a whole generation got hooked on work

Helen Trinca &
Catherine Fox

RANDOM HOUSE AUSTRALIA

Every effort has been made to identify individual permission holders. The publishers would be pleased to hear from any copyright holders who have not been acknowledged.

Random House Australia Pty Ltd
20 Alfred Street, Milsons Point, NSW 2061
http://www.randomhouse.com.au

Sydney   New York   Toronto
London   Auckland   Johannesburg

First published by Random House Australia 2004

National Library of Australia
Cataloguing-in-Publication Entry

Trinca, Helen.
Better than sex: how a whole generation got hooked on work.

  Bibliography.
  ISBN 1 74051 196 4.

  1. Quality of work life. 2. Workaholism. 3. Work and family. I. Fox, Catherine (Catherine Louise). II. Title.

306.361

Cover illustration courtesy Getty Images
Cover design by Nanette Backhouse
Typeset in 12.5/16 pt Adobe Garamond by Midland Typesetters, Maryborough, Victoria
Printed and bound by Griffin Press, Netley, South Australia

10 9 8 7 6 5 4 3 2 1

To our fathers, John Francis Fox (1921–2002)
and Anselmo Trinca (1910–1973)

Contents

Introduction

WHEN WE WERE LITTLE GIRLS, growing up in suburbs at opposite ends of the country, it was our parents who showed us what work was about. In Sydney, one father drove to the office every morning and spent his days on slightly mysterious but important work as a chemical engineer. In Perth, the other father had a smallholding where he ran a poultry farm. He stayed home all day but went up to the sheds before 7 a.m. for equally important toil. Both of our dads worked hard and carried the financial responsibility for their families. In each case there were four children to feed, clothe and school, and our fathers were uncomplaining in their commitment to the task. It's only now, some decades later, as we have talked about this book, that we've realised that neither of them was especially captivated by work. Swapping stories about our fathers, what emerges is a picture of men, both born in the early part of the twentieth century, who would really, truly have preferred to have been off drinking red wine, reading books, travelling the world, social-ising and having adventures. Work brought them some satisfaction and they kept at it. But they never had any doubt that it came second to real life. The notion of work as an end in itself or a major motivating force in their lives was foreign to them. You worked because you had to and, if you were lucky, you got some of the things you wanted. The farmer dad hated authority so was delighted that at the age of forty, he had saved enough to get his own five-acre plot and set up his own farm. He would not make a lot of money but no one could tell him what to do now. The engineer dad loved ideas and the friendship of colleagues. Yes, there were great pleasures to be had from work, if you were lucky, but holidays were more fun.

We have told each other many stories about the way our fathers and mothers approached work when we were young. We've been interested in how our own attitudes to work have been formed, interested to discover how much influence those early role models had on us. We've talked about our mothers and their huge capacity for running households. The farmer's wife worked outside on the farm as well; the other mother spent much of her time in school and community groups. Every now and then, we would get a flash, a memory of how their attitudes towards work and duty and obligation had impacted on us, and where, in particular, the worker genes had come from.

But at times, talking about the way our parents tackled their working lives, it felt like another country, so different is our land-scape and our expectations about what work can deliver. We've got a double interest in the subject. Not only do we work at a time in history when it occupies a central place in our culture, but our jobs involve writing about work. Even more than our colleagues on different journalistic beats or people in different fields, we are our own guinea pigs, our own controlled experiment.

And like all workers, every day at the office gives us so much raw material, the hard bit is to know where to start in describing an area where we are all experts. Then there's the tone. Take your pick – from the brow-beaten cynicism of *Dilbert* to the boosterism of flash mags like *Fast Company*, there are plenty of ways to talk about what work is like right now.

Everyone has a position on work, but as journalists who write on this subject we figured we had better credentials than many to look at the way it dominates our lives and our spirits as never before. For the past few years, our job has been to investigate and describe what is happening in companies and organisations in Australia and overseas. Our focus has been the big end of town, the corporations where work is being reshaped by globalisation and new technology and where working hard and long has taken on a whole new meaning.

As we have looked at the cultural and structural changes in workplaces over the past couple of decades, one idea is constantly reinforced. Work is now at the centre of people's lives; it's the thing they do to make money *and* meaning. Work cannot compete with sex for glamour, excitement and emotion, but it's close. Just as importantly, it can drain people of the energy, time and desire that make sex and intimacy happen. It can push away love, deaden our interest in others and flatten our horizons – and yet still rate as the most important part of our life. For many people work life is more fulfilling, empowering, consistent and controllable than their sex life. Better, in so many ways. A new generation works over the old arguments about work/life balance, shorter hours, longer hours, childcare, flexible shifts. It is important stuff and can easily raise temperatures and launch impassioned discussion. But for many people now there is no longer an argument about *whether* work should determine how we live. Instead we debate *how* work should be managed.

Hooked on work. Not all of us, and not all the time. But in the past decade work galloped ahead of other priorities for many of us. Suddenly it's fine to admit that work means a lot to us, that we like our jobs, that we sometimes feel more complete and integrated at work than in our private lives. Society shares that view. Feel good about your work? Look forward to getting to work so you can get stuck into it all again after the weekend? Once you would have been embarrassed to admit to embracing work as more interesting and engaging than other parts of your life. But today, it's easy. You're in good company.

For us, work has long been a central part of our lives, although we come at it from slightly different perspectives. Knowing we could do the job well, enjoying the power, the sense of personal control, knowing our way around the issues; this was all important to us. But work is much more than that: it is a key part of our identities.

Work imposes routines and disciplines that do not come naturally but which bring security and self-esteem, as well as money. There are many times we'd rather stay home and read a novel, bake a cake, go to the movies, just hang. Yet the requirement of regular commitments of energy to our employers has not been so onerous that it has made us unhappy. We have been frustrated and disappointed: sometimes the anger has been directed at the boss and the system, sometimes at our own failure to handle stress or challenges. But over the years, the more dominant emotion has been the thrill of achievement. Looking back, the daily mistakes and problems are moderated by a sense of enjoyment in our work.

One day, early in our conversations around writing this book, we asked each other what was truly important about work. It was fascinating that we volunteered similar statements about the *process* of journalism. We'd loved the research, the writing, the practice of our craft. That had been as important as any published article. We also confessed to something that we had found difficult to articulate in the past – that we had enjoyed peak experiences around work. Sometimes when it had all come together, we had felt inspired and empowered. There were times when work had blocked out everything else. That day, we also admitted that we had been secretive, at times even slightly ashamed of how much work meant to us. In the early parts of our careers, especially, we knew that talking up work labelled you as a bit of a loser or, conversely, far too ambitious. Not a good look.

It was towards the end of the 1990s that we found ourselves writing about work from the perspective of management theory, sociology and behaviour. It was the decade when newspapers began to look for a new approach to covering the topic – moving away from straight business coverage and away from the reporting of work through the lens of the union movement and traditional industrial relations practice. We became immersed in the question of how work was organised, how companies ran their operations and the way power functioned in offices. We were increasingly interested in work as a concept, something that was bigger than the job.

Today work is cool, but it was not always so. In the 1960s, for example, popular culture questioned existing power: work was for middle-aged men who could not see they had a choice of freedom. If you were young and working, you were either in a temporary space before you found your true calling; you were in it for the money (generally to fund an overseas holiday); or you were work-ing in a profession where the goal was service to others, not to your employer. The prevailing belief among the younger generation was that if you were going to really throw yourself into work, it should be for a greater cause than the work itself. It was incumbent on you to find a vocation that had meaning. If you couldn't do that, then it was more or less your duty to drop out. This was at a time when Australian governments ran large public service departments across the country and when private companies were less important. The corporate world exerted far less influence on our culture and how we saw work and ourselves.

Those attitudes drifted over into the next decade. It was a beautiful thing to start a career in the early 1970s, as one of us did. Fresh from university, you answered a job advertisement or two, assumed you'd get both and took it from there. Work was a short-term proposition: you couldn't imagine staying in the same job for very long and knew that if you left one position you would quickly find another. There was almost full employment in Australia and it was easy to question the value of working for the man and argue that real life and meaning lay somewhere else, like a working holiday in London or helping the poor in developing countries.

By the 1980s, work was less about remaking the world and more about making money. Jobs became far harder to get. The oil shock of 1973 changed the way young Australians thought about jobs: it was much harder to get one and once in the workforce, there was more incentive to stay. When one of us began our career in 1981, jobs were scarce in journalism, in fact anywhere. Competition was fierce for new entrants and it was a good idea to work hard. It would get even tougher in the next few years and by the end of the decade, it was very clear that even industriousness would not protect you from large-scale sackings across the economy. By the 1990s, workers in the West understood that the project was tricky and came with mixed messages – buy into the system but don't trust it too much.

Many of those attitudes continue to shape the way we work today, but something else happened in the 1990s: along with the distrust, work moved to centre stage and became an end in itself. It was the decade when work was offered to us as a pleasure, as the space where you could be most fulfilled. Family was no longer enough. Religion failed the test of meaning for many. The environment, the natural world, had many delights and was rediscovered by many people as it came increasingly under threat. But nature was hard to integrate into the requirement to work and exploit resources in order to survive. Work was the thing which would make life worthwhile: work was crucial to survival, both physically and emotionally.

By the time we sat down to write this book, we knew something was going on around the world of work which was turning it into the number one influence in the lives of many people. We knew this enthusiasm for the work project did not resonate with everyone. We knew we were privileged and that for many people work remained a trial which gave them little more than a wage. But running parallel with the exhaustion and long hours in the workplace there was a sense of excitement and purpose about work. It seemed that many people felt real at work, where life was sometimes smoother than at home. Though there were times when you dreaded the dawn of a new working day, mornings when you would 'wake up and throw up' at the very thought of going to the office, in general work was a no-brainer. It made sense, even with all its contradictions of stress and satisfaction.

Twenty years ago, aspiring urbanites might ask someone they met at a party where they went to school. Today, they ask what someone does for a living. We are our work, at least in the public sphere, and at home, work continues to define our families and us. How long is it since you've seen a woman in an apron in a television ad? Today's ads set in the home are more likely to feature young women dressed for the office than for a half-hour at the stove. Like the soaps and dramas on television, ads are inhabited by women and men for whom work is a major preoccupation.

Thirty years ago when married women, by and large, did not work outside the home full-time or even part-time, those ads were very different. Unrealistic too. Most of us had never seen such expansive, clean aprons as those sported by television's laundering, polishing mothers. But they were right to ignore the office and factory. Men, and they were overwhelmingly men, went to work and worked hard but a job was only part of their identity. The footy, golf club, the family and church helped fill out the picture.

Now that every adult is presumed to be ready, willing and available for paid labour, work is at the centre of life. We feel like failures if we can't get satisfaction from our job. It is no longer enough simply to have a sound, well-paid position. It must give purpose and meaning. If you clock off psychologically, it means you don't get it. Work has colonised our lives, and the organisation is more influential in our society than ever. Many of us are now deeply absorbed in the work project, prepared to pay the price in time lost from family and relationships, the thinning of our community and public lives. Our parents' generation knew work as a very different power. They faced setbacks in their jobs and made compromises in order to make enough money to provide for their families. But, as we noted earlier, they did not seem to be as absorbed by work as we are.

It's no coincidence that this immersion in work is happening as technology revolutionises the world. It's a given that we take work home sometimes, now that the internet and the mobile phone make it so easy. We live in a world where we can't get enough of the information available through the World Wide Web and a 24/7 approach to communications and news. The lines between work and play are blurred. In our cities, workers sip lattes at 11 a.m. as they talk to clients or do some paperwork. When they leave the office, they might go bowling with their work colleagues, or out for an evening where the drinks and food are subsidised by the company. When they get home they check their emails, perhaps complete a report and finally go to bed. Work is not only about long hours but is a seamless connection of time on and off the job.

Looking back, we have clear images of our fathers being very different when they weren't working: more relaxed, more 'themselves'. Today, that distinction is disappearing: employers want us to be creative at work, consultants urge us to bring the 'whole person' to the office. The ideal is for public and private lives to merge as a way of bringing maximum and effective energy to the workplace. It's seductive, this notion of being authentic in the office, but as academic, writer and former Clinton Secretary of Labor, Robert Reich, says in *The Future of Success*, 'constantly being on – creating, teaching, convincing and selling – can be emotionally draining'.[1] Even when we're not at work we find there's not much emotional or intellectual space left for our non-work lives.

Work has always been a way of creating ourselves. In *My Job, My Self*, Al Gini says that 'work is the means by which we form our character and complete ourselves as people'.[2] Professor Amanda Sinclair of the Melbourne Business School says that work may be the only thing that answers the question of why we are here.[3] The problem for some people is that work in the twenty-first century is so narrowly described – as paid work, largely carried out in someone else's space at someone else's behest. The only activity that really seems to define the individual is paid work. For many people though, the importance of work is no longer open to argument. Unpaid work at home, with children or in the community is useful but not central to identity. Women have cottoned on to that one: there is no glamour or kudos attached to staying home with the kids. Your only chance of exerting power – even within a marriage – is to be able to bring your own economic contribution to the table and to be part of that wider world. Work gives you individual buying power and access to the modern attractions of our consumer culture.

Many commentators are horrified by this focus, afraid of what it means to our humanity, our ability to connect with others in anything other than an instrumentalist fashion. There have been many books decrying the workaholism of our age. At the other end of the spectrum are the books straining with enthusiasm about the joy of work and the empowerment of the modern employee. Neither of these positions seems to us to be very useful and while we have at times been caught up in arguing each scenario, we increasingly feel that they tell only part of the story.

We are under no illusions: work can be very hard and there is plenty of evidence of toxic workplaces, narcissistic bosses and oppressed workers. We don't make light of these as there have been many times when we have found our companies and our bosses less than fair and less than competent. And plenty of times too, as managers, when we have got it wrong. We have compromised and navigated the system just like millions of others do every day. There have been times when we have worked too hard, ignoring those close to us, totally focused on and driven by whatever project or assignment we have been on. At times we have made choices around work and suffered consequences that we regret. But we gained enormously – financially, emotionally and intellectually – from that intense commitment. Was it tough? Yes. Was it all bad? No way. Were we driven to work by our bosses, victims of capitalism? Well, we find it hard to see it that way, knowing the levels of satisfaction we gained from work.

Does everyone share this enthusiasm? Does work do it for everyone? Clearly not. Which is why we find the opposite view of work – as joyous project – hard to accept. For many people, the rah rah atmosphere pushed by some management literature is simply ludicrous. Anyone who's ever been a paid worker, and that's most of us, knows that there's something wrong with that picture.

Better Than Sex does something different. It's a reality check on what work means now and a glimpse at where it's going. Writing the book has proved fascinating and revealing. The moment is right for a review and preview. The start of a new century is a good time to look at the system and understand what drives us to work. In recent years, as journalists, we have had access to the leaders of the biggest companies in Australia and we have spent time talking to people at many levels of organisations across the globe, whose role is to build, manage and mould the workspace.

We are interested in looking beyond the slog to see why it is that we allow work to be so powerful. We want to understand why people feel like winners, not losers, when they spend long hours in the office, why they put work ahead of family, religion and leisure and make it the main measure of human value. We recognise the financial pressure on people to stick with jobs they dislike and the emotional pressure to succeed by holding a top, well-paid job. It's naïve to think we are free agents in all of this or to believe the management texts which suggest workers can create their own jobs and their own personas at work. Only to a point, we would argue.

Even in our working lives, we've been part of a revolution around work, one which we would not have expected. Today the intensity of the workplace runs hand in hand with an intense debate on the politics of work, the government policies that may or may not impact on our working lives, and a huge stream of management literature and thought directed at shaping work and workers. It is an extraordinary period in the history of work, and this book is about trying to understand how we got here and where we are going with the work project.

In the first section, we look at how the 1990s transformed the way workplaces operate and how we think about work. Our consumption of work, we argue, is part of the work ethic and a key human driver. We argue too that the 1990s saw a huge shift away from powerful unions to individuals who expect to negotiate their own way through the workplace. The organisation has emerged strongly but pressure from a well educated, highly individualistic workforce continues to challenge the way workplaces operate.

In the second section, we dig deeper into the way companies attempt to mould the workplace, and their interest in finding the perfect worker with correct attitudes and the right level of ambition. Here we see the tension between individuals and organisations, between creativity and control, between work and family demands. Measuring output, defining and encouraging the right behaviour for a productive workplace and owning the hearts and minds of workers are more important than ever to corporations. It's a trend that seems to grow as workers try to sort out a balance between private and public lives.

In the final section of the book, we look at the current thinking on organisations and where they are headed. What should individual workers do to remodel the contract and find their way through the maze of the workplace? And finally, what will happen to us as people as well as workers? How can we mould our identities and shape them to make sense of a work culture which demands high emotional commitment as the price for our physical survival?

Better Than Sex is for anyone interested in or puzzled by the way work dominates our lives. There are no pat answers, but exploring the complexities around the modern work project is remarkably illuminating. Our analysis has moved far beyond our original thesis and uncovered some fresh perspectives. We know that there are some sectors of the economy that we have not covered, some areas we do not understand. Just as we were winding up the book, friends who spent time as retirees in the United Kingdom arrived home, aglow with tales of the robust, lively area of working in the black economy. There is, they told us, an entire sub-culture of people working outside the system – and you're not including them. They are correct, but we make no apologies for focusing on the world of work we know best. These are the organisations that have the most influence on the way that most of us operate, shaping jobs at all levels and dominating the social and community attitudes towards work.

Better Than Sex is, in truth, an outrageous title for a book about work, but it seems to capture a certain brio we felt about this project. We wanted to write a book that demonstrated the power of work without sinking into a sombre critique of its oppressive, inhuman qualities. So many books on work leave you clawing the walls in desperation, wondering how any of us can ever enjoy our jobs. We reckon there's more than that to the debate about work in the twenty-first century.

---

1. Reich, Robert. *The Future of Success*. Vintage, 2002, p. 217.
2. Gini, Al. *My Job, My Self: Work and the Creation of the Modern Individual*. Routledge, 2001, p. 2.
3. Interview with Professor Amanda Sinclair.

1

The way we work now

WE WORK IN A SWISH HIGH-RISE building in central Sydney. It's a far cry from the grimy rabbit warrens of the newspaper offices of our past. Those offices – News Limited, on the edge of the CBD near Central railway station, and Fairfax, a little further along the ugly, frenetic stretch of Sydney that becomes Parramatta Road – were legendary for their lack of gloss and aesthetic appeal. They were unattractive workplaces in many ways though they made a sort of statement about the role of newspapers and the journalistic Fourth Estate, about sitting on the edge of society, looking in as critics. Whatever. Today the buildings have been transformed by modern refits yet the memories of a time when our working environment was very different still linger.

The Fairfax empire is now slap bang in the middle of a vibrant city and our office is high up on the twenty-fifth floor. It looks very much like the premises of any other corporation. When we head out to interview someone at the blue-chip management consultants

McKinsey & Company or at one of the banks or investment houses, we are in familiar territory. It's a seamless fit from our world to theirs these days. For some at Fairfax, there are brilliant views across Darling Harbour to Balmain and beyond, and downstairs we can mix with other denizens of the building: the creatives from John Singleton's ad agency, the auditors and consultants from Price-waterhouseCoopers or the marketers and managers from Nestlé and IBM.

We can sit about in leather armchairs on the ground floor, drinking coffee from the bars scattered through the complex. Around us, on an average mid-morning, are dozens of other workers. Some are deep in conversation, documents open on the low tables in front of them. Others talk or send text messages on mobile phones. Some are visitors, delighted by the chance to walk through the complex and treat it like an indoor street where the lines between public and private spaces blur. Designed by the famous architect Harry Seidler, it is emblematic of the fuzzy line between work and play, between formal hours spent at the desk and time out at the coffee shop.

This is a building where corporate life is played out. It is also a place where life and work collide and where one is no longer quar-antined from the other. The workers wandering about downstairs in our building are not on their lunchbreaks but neither are they skiving off. Some are meeting clients or contacts in a more relaxed atmosphere. When they go upstairs, they are unlikely to have a separate office to conduct meetings in. Some are hot-deskers who have no permanent area of their own and stack their papers and files in a drawer at the end of the corridor. Typing on their laptops in the foyer is all part of the working day.

Others lolling about downstairs just want to have fun as well as get the job done and see the coffee break as a regular part of the 24/7 approach they take to their jobs. Conventionally, most of them would be upstairs, heads down, under the boss's eye and focused on their appointed tasks. Conventionally too, they would be out the door at 5 p.m., with enough energy left for the other half of their lives and no requirement to respond to a client's phone call or to finesse that PowerPoint presentation for Thursday's meeting.

That's not the way it is for many workers now. Today's CBD workplaces are about getting a good coffee in the lobby as well as getting in on time upstairs. We're not suggesting that work in the twenty-first century has become the fun-filled exercise touted during the years of Silicon Valley hype in the 1990s. Sometimes, as we hurry to work through the city streets, it's plain that the routines and restrictions of the company make work an endurance test for some people, or, at best, a bore. Those contradictions are now part of the landscape of work, whether you are in a slick CBD environment or a suburban conveyancing office, whether you're a 'knowledge worker' based in Broome or you are navigating your way through the services sector as a middle manager in a hotel on the Gold Coast. Our example of how our newspaper offices were 'corporatised' is specific to industry, time and place and is not necessarily representative. Our companies were slow to modernise. If you look at old black and white movies set in the Manhattan of the 1940s or 1950s, you can see that the notion of sleek office space is nothing new.

As well, many Australians work outside our narrow workspace. We know that not every sector has the licence we have long enjoyed as journalists. In Australia's factories, work is far more regimented, with employees held to strict break times and with little chance to leave work to pick up the dry cleaning or run to the ATM. In retail outlets or telephone call centres you can't suddenly down tools and meet for a latte. For people in the service sector who are positioned at front counters working with the public, there is not much opportunity to shape the day to your own rhythm. But wherever you work you will find common ground with others over the many paradoxes between freedom and restriction, informality and control. You will find managers monitoring your performance on one hand, and on the other, encouraging you to accept individual responsibility. The boss sits in an open-plan office where he or she is overtly 'of the people' yet everyone knows there are precise rules about how power is dispensed.

Perhaps the biggest paradox is the sense that many of us are on the job even when not physically present at the office. This is one of the big shifts in the way we see work. It's not accidental, of course. Imagine if your job is to produce a batch of perfect T-shirts at a factory. There's not much point worrying about it at weekends, but if the aim is to come up with a perfect marketing or business plan for the T-shirt that is mass-produced in China, you can think about it right through to Sunday evening and beyond. As work has become more detached from machines or physical products, it has become more integrated into our lives. You can keep thinking about a work-related problem when you're on the train going home, or doing laps at the pool before work. It means that, for better or worse, much of your work is portable. The 24/7 life is not just about the long hours in the office but also about the time spent thinking about the office when you're at home.

Away from the job, work is often still our main topic of conversation. Workers complain about how much pressure they are under and about the hungry job that eats up all their waking hours. Talking about long hours and the intensity of work is a constant across age groups and social classes. These trends are portrayed as frightening and soul-destroying, yet work is compelling for many. To work long hours is almost a badge of honour in a society that reveres achievement and success. To admit that you are not busy suggests you are not interested in the main games of status and consumption. Home at 6 p.m.? My, my, my!

Some of this is self-imposed. Many of us drive ourselves to work harder and self-supervise this effort. French philosopher and social theorist Michel Foucault showed how in modern societies, institutional discipline is not achieved through brute force or direct coercion but by getting people to internalise commitment and discipline. We don't necessarily need to be closely controlled or supervised in order to work hard because the ideals that might once have been imposed on us are now part of our very identity. Everyone takes responsibility for getting the job done. The boss burns the midnight oil but so do the troops.

'It's "why should I whip you when I can get you to whip yourself?",' says Carl Rhodes, a researcher in organisational learning at the University of Technology, Sydney.[1] Even the peak union body, the ACTU, which has campaigned staunchly against long hours and unpaid overtime, recognises the role employees play in propping up the culture. 'The culture of long hours is something that is far more complex than simply telling workers they have to work long hours against their will,' says ACTU assistant secretary Richard Marles. 'It's a culture that has been bought into by working people.'[2] This is especially the case among professional and white-collar workers whose work can overflow into the rest of their lives.

It adds up to a workforce and workplaces that are quite different from those that reigned supreme in the decades after the Second World War, at a time of regulated national economies and relatively limited technology. Back then, workers had little mobility. Managers might be sent interstate or to rural Australia to run a branch, but the idea of working across nations and time zones was alien. Australian workers rarely made an interstate telephone call on the job, let alone an international one, and technology was something taught in tech schools, not something you used at the office. Even twenty years ago, the fax machine was a revolution, allowing companies an alternative to physically moving documents around traffic-jammed cities or halfway across the world. Today, of course, the fax is almost an anachronism in a workplace where everyone is on the Net.

Employees have become their own secretaries thanks to Power-Point and email. Even managers must process their own reports, do their own correspondence and photocopying, organise a data bank, as well as plan strategies and pitch to clients. Technology has made workers at all levels more directly responsible for tasks previously handled by secretaries or the typing pool. It has also helped to make offices very speedy places. Reports are generated rapidly and updated and amended quickly. The whole complex system of proofing and retyping by an assistant has disappeared. Documents that used to take days or weeks to be published now appear in hours. Tasks that were previously divided between many people holding different positions have been condensed into one. People juggle many different skills every day. The tasks may not be especially complex but they often involve technology.

Multi-skilling, which began as a way to end unproductive demarcation lines between people working alongside each other, is now a natural part of white-collar jobs, forced on employees as corporations slashed support staff in the 1980s and 1990s. In his 2001 book, *Slack: Getting Past Busywork, Burnout, and the Myth of Total Efficiency*, American management consultant Tom DeMarco suggested companies had overdone the downsizing and outsourcing and needed to hire back some clerical support. The notion of highly paid managers doing their own photocopying and typing suggested a corporate obsession with efficiency had gone too far. But his ideas already sound dated: everyone is techno-literate now and most of us would not have it any other way. Technology has been stimulating, exciting and liberating on many levels.

PowerPoint has changed the way information is presented and ideas are developed. Some believe it's actually changed the way an emerging generation thinks. As journalists working in business, we were initially horrified when we saw PowerPoint spread like an oil slick across meetings and conferences. The ideas presented often seemed banal and obvious, and the PowerPoint presentation little more than a toy for presenting them in a very simplistic form. PowerPoint could make the most inane report or pitch look more sophisticated as the dot points took on a gravitas all their own.

There's a similar danger in email, which drives the work pattern in many companies. It's an incredible communication tool and streamlines operations, but it means workers are sometimes hesitant to pick up the phone to sort something out with a colleague or client, preferring instead to swap five or six emails. And not everyone has fallen into line. A couple of years back, Roger Corbett, the CEO of Woolworths, explained to us that he tries to bypass emails when he can and talk to people on the phone.[3] It meant faster decisions, he said. Our own newspaper office has been transformed by email, with the great bulk of work now dependent in some way on this technology.

Email also changes the way people respond to questions or proposals. You feel strong pressure to hit the 'Reply' button immediately and acknowledge a message, promising that you will consider it and get back in touch later. Sometimes you do but often the thinking stops with the reply and queries are left unanswered as employees move on to the next message. There's speed and activity, but not necessarily progress or productive work. And worst of all, email creates a very heavy workload for conscientious workers. Who hasn't returned from a holiday to find dozens, perhaps hundreds of emails shouting for attention? Sometimes there seems no way out from under the stack of messages in your inbox. Some workers have developed defensive strategies, sending automatic replies to emails which state that not all messages can be dealt with. Even so, there's an awful lot of screening to do every day – the sort of screening that support staff once carried out.

The World Wide Web is also deeply entrenched in work patterns, especially for white-collar workers who are online permanently via their PCs. They spend their days connected to a huge bank of information, games, pornography, gambling, romance and job sites, a world of amazing promise as a research and communication tool but also a potential distraction and time waster. Some companies have tried to limit the time workers spend surfing the Net by blocking access to specific sites outside of the lunchbreak. At the Australian Broadcasting Corporation a sign pops up on internet sites deemed inappropriate for employees to browse. But overall, online usage is difficult to police and monitoring signals a lack of trust. Some companies have now realised that allowing employees to wander the Web is not necessarily a waste of time for knowledge workers who stay ahead by staying connected.[4]

The growth of the Web and email have helped blur the line between public and private space. One moment a middle manager is checking the company Intranet to review the salary levels of junior staff, the next he is booking a cheap holiday in Hawaii online. In all these ways the technology reinforces our connections with work because the tools we use at work are the same tools we use for play or conducting domestic business.

Technology that forces us to be available for work even when at home has been used by organisations and companies to colonise the home for work purposes. The process works the other way as well and the workplace is now deeply affected by the personal, with the main tools once again being the mobile phone and the internet. As more and more women work, many home tasks are carried out at work. Once it was shocking, and possibly a sackable offence, to ring a tradesman from the office to make an appointment, call up the curtain shop to get a quote on some new curtains, telephone a friend to check on her wellbeing, or even interrogate your tax accountant. All these calls would once have been regarded as relating to personal matters. They should be attended to outside working hours or delegated to those not in paid work. But now that almost everyone works, how do we run the rest of our lives if we can't make these sorts of inquiries during business hours? Today men and women, married or single, childless or with families, use the hours at work for a host of activities that would not have been allowed a few decades ago. Necessity has made it so. And sometimes there's a conscious trade-off – if you work at weekends, why not call the accountant on Monday morning?

For most office-based workers, email starts the day. It's the new message bank, the technology that allows people to keep working, sending messages late into the night for immediate attention the next morning.

'I get in around 7.30,' says Nancy Milne, at that stage a partner in a major law firm in Sydney. 'Then I go through the overnight email, look at the diary, do the running list for what's on the agenda that day.'[5] Her PA will not be in until 9 a.m., so Milne spends that hour and a half getting organised for when the rest of the world comes to work. She might get on the Net or do some research. Some of her clients know she is in early so they call or email her.

For workers like long-distance transport operators, bus or train drivers, tradespeople and builders, or people who work in sales outside of an office environment, technology has had a dramatic impact on their operations. These workers can't log on to the Net as they drive around the city, but they are plugged in via their mobile phones. Think about the relative isolation of the bus driver from head office or family in the days before the mobile. And what of the plumber who needed a helper back in the office to take the calls while he was out on the job? Now a tradesman can take bookings and offer quotes throughout the day, thanks to technology.

Technology has also created an even playing field at the office when it comes to information – increasingly, everyone sees the news at the same time and gets on to the Net for the same material. Employees can all send an email to the boss, and they don't have to wait till they're senior enough to get a private audience. Chief executive officers at companies such as ANZ and BHP have spoken to the media about the time they spend answering regular emails from staff. In some corporations email has helped break down the barriers between the executives and workers, and much of the mystique around the boss has collapsed. Many workers know what the bosses do, and sometimes it seems they don't do much that the more junior staff couldn't do themselves. Email means that they can communicate directly with the chief, something which would have been impossible a few years back.

The technology transformation at work has helped trigger a shift in power. In fact some of today's bosses now look more like project managers or coordinators who must negotiate with workers rather than order them about. Even people just joining the workforce are likely to discuss directions, not just take them. 'Baby boomer' bosses talk about the changes they are experiencing in terms of power and authority but they take it for granted that they must approach staff, especially younger staff, in a different way now. As journalists, we have worked in pretty informal offices. Years ago Sir Larry Lamb, a British media executive who for a short time was editor of *The Australian*, amazed the staff there when he insisted on being called Sir Larry, rather than Larry. Even the cadets and teenagers who ran the messages, the copy-boys and girls, were on first-name terms with the editors.

In many offices in the past the lines of authority were more distinct. The boss hid behind his secretary, positioned in the outer office. Sightings were rare, which only added to the mystery. White-collar workers did not face rigid and repetitive work on the assembly line, but many still clocked on, observed strict rules about physical movement during the day, stuck to regular meal breaks and generally asked permission before leaving the work-space. Authority was taken for granted.

Walk into an office today and it's hard to tell who the juniors are. The hierarchy may have been reduced but now every twenty-something reckons they should be the boss. The new recruit surprises you with a language based on achieving outcomes and managing the system. Gone is the sense that the boss or company will take your career in hand: the pressure is on each person to develop a strategy for success and navigate the people and the pitfalls around you. Little wonder that the junior sales rep is likely to have just read the latest book on how to 'manage up' and is already one step ahead of her supervisor.

Deference is out as employees treat all comers as equals. Business coach John Vamos says there's a new generation unmoved by directions from traditional authority figures. 'Somewhere in the fabric, age and experience were eliminated as the natural basis of authority,' he says.[6] This generation takes a different position towards the boss and is more inclined to want to discuss an issue. Prospective employees will ask for information and then decide whether or not to join up.

Chris Fogarty, group manager, marketing operations at Allens Arthur Robinson, one of Australia's biggest law firms, used to be able to assign a task and assume it would be done. Now Fogarty often finds himself negotiating with employees about which tasks they prefer to do.[7] It's a story you hear over and over from managers in an age when authority is now mediated differently and more employees feel able to question the allocation of tasks.

As team-based and project work increases, workers feel they

have a choice about whether they will sign up to an exercise; some are even courted to come on board. The team explicitly involves a very different power relationship between members than was present in more conventional arrangements where duties were handed down a line. It's also the case that the demand for more equal power in the workplace has forced new ways of working. Teams are the result, as much as the cause, of a more egalitarian environment.

Teams cut across departments or units, so that you may feel more affinity with or loyalty to team members rather than the person sitting next to you in your department. These new relationships are often much stronger than any attachment to the firm and can form a set of personal networks which endure. In his book *Free Agent Nation*, American commentator Daniel Pink talks about the strength of alliances between colleagues who work in different firms. These alliances are often the strongest links between people, so that when an employee leaves a company, it is to that informal network that he or she looks for the next job or project. The relationships outlive the jobs and give knowledge workers a different sort of negotiating power, one based on the network, not the company.[8]

Workers across the board have all been affected by decades of change around authority and this has had a big impact on the workplace. Popular culture, marketing and advertising, as well as philosophy and psychology, have reinforced ideas concerning personal empowerment. An entire generation has moved through self-help books and encounter groups to take it for granted that they have rights to self-expression and self-actualisation. Today's employees might have to put their heads down when times are tough and they fear for their jobs but they have vastly different views on authority than their parents had at a similar age.

When William H. Whyte wrote *The Organization Man* in

1956, he described a generation of young Americans who were too malleable, too quiescent to the organisation. 'The well-functioning team is a whole greater than the sum of its parts, yes – all this is indeed true,' he wrote. 'But is it the truth that now needs belaboring? Precisely because it is an age of organisation, it is the other side of the coin that needs emphasis. We do need to know how to co-operate with The Organization but, more than ever, so do we need to know how to resist it.'[9] Today many workers are employed by very large organisations and continue to conform, but at a more personal level – with managers and colleagues – they will often strongly question authority. Today's employees have a sense of themselves as individuals, able to challenge the boss.

And companies often have to go along with that change. They need committed workers more than ever. Peter Drucker, the elder statesman of management practice and theory who is now in his nineties, was the first to really understand just how much life would change for both managers and workers. In an essay in *The Atlantic Monthly* in 1999 he warned that knowledge workers were the key to the global economy. Employers would have to 'attract, hold and motivate knowledge workers' if they were to stay profitable. In the end, it would mean 'satisfying their values and giving them social recognition and social power. It will have to be done by turning them from subordinates into fellow executives, and from employees, however well-paid, into partners.'[10] It's not easy to institute the Drucker approach but some organisations in Australia, such as the CSIRO, have begun the process. Some have employed 'knowledge management' leaders whose job is to try looking at the organisation and its talent in a new way. At the legal firm Minter Ellison, David Rymer carries the title of Director of Know-How. Rymer says the downside of empowering workers in this way is that it blurs the line between work and the rest of life, with employees often tempted to take a 24/7 approach. And while it can mean the end of formal hierarchy, a knowledge management approach creates a different sort of hierarchy as people become 'experts' and think of themselves differently.[11]

Susan Annunzio, an American who runs the Centre for High Performance within the recruitment firm TMP/Hudson, has found that employers will often try to *instruct* their most talented staff to come up with ideas.[12] They get them together for a meeting and announce that the new world order will be around creativity and innovation and ideas – and then expect a result. It doesn't work, of course, and the modern boss has to find other ways to achieve buy-in from even their most talented employees. Bain and Company chair Orit Gadish warns there are a hundred different ways for an employee to say 'yes' to a directive but in fact mean 'no'.[13] Anyone who has worked in a large organisation has seen how middle managers can agree to a new process or structure and then simply fail to implement it within their own unit or division. They tell the boss that it's all on track but simply shove the document in the bottom drawer.

This passive resistance can be as difficult to manage as outright rejection of a direction. Work in the knowledge economy is hard to define and getting people to do what you want them to do requires a sophisticated understanding of human psychology.

The recruitment and consulting industries have warned companies that they must change their ways if they are to attract the top people who will give them the edge in a very competitive business environment. Companies increasingly see themselves as locked into a 'war for talent', to snare the best and brightest in a period when the demand from shareholders for profits has rarely been more intense. The message is: you need to approach the hiring process in a fresh way. Rather than interviewing these elite candidates, managers must be prepared to be interviewed *by* the candidates. The mantra of the 1990s was that good knowledge workers were in short supply and could choose their employer, not the other way around. There was more than a touch of hyperbole in this idea that the employee was as powerful as the boss. But 'war for talent', a concept developed by McKinsey & Company in the 1990s, tapped into the empowerment mood of the decade. Later, as big corporations collapsed, 'war for talent' was sneered at by many who blamed these failures on employees with big ideas and no skills at implementation. For some companies, the demise of this war was a relief. Perhaps those knowledge workers were not so powerful after all.

But information is power and easy access to that information through channels like the Internet has forced business to hand over some of its control to workers in order to function in an information age. It is impossible for any boss or manager to hoard information or knowledge in the way they could thirty or forty years ago. An office cannot operate without email being available to all. If all messaging had to go through the boss, a company would be paralysed. But this open approach to information and the 'democratisation' of data gives workers their own power and can lead to a less malleable workforce. The information-rich worker is less likely to conform to the regimen of an office or workshop. However, this potential threat to the power of the boss has been reduced by the way we have internalised many values that once had to be enforced. Everyone at work is their own boss now, driving themselves to succeed, keeping up to the mark, toiling when nobody is watching. Employees have absorbed the messages and values of the company and the system so well that they happily supervise themselves. The information that has empowered us on the one hand has been countered by the way we have internalised an ethos of achievement.

Not everyone working in a knowledge economy works to this 'inner boss'. Solicitors are among the most elite and well-paid professionals but have very clear external governors which enforce a strict, performance-based culture. It is extraordinary that these professionals are so constrained, forced to reach quotas of 'billable hours' every day if they want to survive and succeed. They are given little freedom to run their own show, listen to their own inner clocks or work in a more fluid manner. The lawyer is measured every day in a system that would have made Henry Ford very happy. In this sense, lawyers have become their own accountants.

Many workplaces used to run on a kind of hidden momentum that could often be very effective but was not transparent. In today's workplace, there is little room for such serendipity and no place to hide when it comes to explaining what you are doing. It is another paradox of modern work that this requirement to document your plans and then tick the boxes when you have accomplished these tasks has become popular precisely at a time when jobs are increasingly about intangible knowledge.

In what is often now termed the 'weightless' economy, much of work has become about ideas. It is often hard to know what the product is, or at least what you've done that has added to its value. Yet workers are asked by managers to be specific about their tasks. This has led to a generation that is expert in stating the blindingly obvious in the most obscure management-speak in an effort to get the boss off their backs. Focus on performance is important but sometimes it collapses into a banal exercise where both worker and manager seem to be involved in a surreal and time-wasting tango. No wonder some workers opt for passive resistance.

This all adds up to employees not often being left alone in the workplace, despite the freedom to enjoy a latte at 11 a.m. Modern employers are preoccupied, sometimes obsessed, with measuring performance and monitoring output. It makes them little different from the early twentieth-century scientific management expert Frederick Winslow Taylor.[14] Taylor's time and motion studies are ridiculed by all but the most anachronistic thinkers, but process management and improvement and efforts to measure output are now taken for granted.

In just a few years, performance reviews have become embedded in Australian companies. How effective they are is cause for much debate and workers are often cynical about their true purpose, arguing that they are not, as management would have it, an opportunity for feedback both ways, but a way for the company to build a file on each worker, a file that can be used to fire rather than promote. This doesn't help the sense of trust that companies are desperate to build. But performance management is an inevitable development in a knowledge economy where companies worry that people will become so powerful and autonomous that they will be hard to control. When they allow employees to give honest feedback on their jobs, performance appraisals are extremely useful. But often they simply help managers tilt the power back in their favour.

Can companies really measure output when the products they are creating are based on intangibles like quality, allure or status? Some workers hate efforts to document their work in this way. Yet if workers want to succeed, there is little choice but to embrace a world where they are referred to as 'assets', a term once applied to a four-tonne truck or a factory.

Talking constantly about employees as assets may depersonalise them but it's not a one-way street. We were struck a few years back when young people in our own workplace used the phrase 'point of difference'. Sometimes they were talking about the product – the newspaper, the magazine – and how it was positioned in the market so that it stood out or offered readers something different. But often they were talking about themselves as products with characteristics that made them more saleable than a competitor. American management guru Tom Peters first preached the 'brand of you' back in the late 1990s and the magazine *Fast Company* built a franchise on the notion that employees should approach their careers as if they were selling themselves. Today, even workers who have never read Peters or the magazine understand that self-promotion and a focus on their strong points are among the most important skills they will learn.

Organisational consultant Viv Read says often employers now exploit that trend for workers to see themselves as individuals who 'sell' their skills to a company. Read runs her own company, Crosstech, in Sydney and has worked in organisations for more than thirty years. In that time she has seen the downside of employee 'empowerment': 'There's a sense in which companies now say: you make your own choices, we make sure you get the information so that you can make the best choices. But that makes some pretty big assumptions that people have got what it takes to make the right choices.'[15]

Is it exploitation or liberation when the apprentice hairdressers at an expensive Sydney salon are required to buy their own hairdryers because the company no longer provides a tool that would once have been part of the shop's fittings? In this example the apprentice is being treated as an independent contractor and he or she must take all the risk of the machinery breaking down. Is it exploitation when applicants for entry into the police force must pay for their own medical checks? Again, the applicant is being treated as someone powerful enough to run a 'tender' for a job, and the medical check is seen as an investment, not a cost. But in reality this approach shifts responsibility back to the worker for processes that were once the responsibility of employers.

The physical and psychological unhitching of workers has been a key trend of the workplace since the 1980s. The idea that you are your most important asset and that you have to focus on building your portfolio of skills is attractive to companies. For a start, it frees employers from providing long-term career structures or training. There has also been a move away from a 'duty of care' to workers beyond the precise legal requirements. Once workers looked to the company to provide long-term security and in return the company expected loyalty and obedience. There was an unspoken bargain in which both sides understood the rules.

Employees aren't the only ones who are being unhitched. Look around an office in the CBD today and you may be hard pressed to find many people who are on staff in the traditional way. The IT experts are contracted in, the PAs are employed by an agency and the person doing the structural reorganisation or running the culture program works for a management consultant. Even the guy sitting down with middle managers to go over strategy is a coach, paid an hourly rate. Twenty or thirty years ago, the idea that you could earn your living from telling companies how to operate or telling them who to hire would have seemed strange. Today it is taken for granted and the advice industry is part of an outsourced business model in which companies employ a basic core of workers, then hire everyone else in on a regular or occasional basis via hire firms or on contract. Even the human resources work is often outsourced to consultants who manage everything from payroll to performance appraisal.

Cindy Luken is a glamorous and lively woman who, in the mid-1990s, set up a successful Australian business producing gourmet biscuits. Her brand, Luken & May (sold in 2003 to distributor Stuart Alexander Australia, although Luken and her team continue to be involved), has been sold in stores like David Jones, four-star hotels and gourmet shops, and overseas in spots like Harvey Nichols in London, as well as Tesco and Sainsbury's supermarkets. Luken's company was small, just a dozen or so people to help design the biscuits and market them. The baking, packaging and distribution were contracted out. Once, someone like Luken would have adopted a traditional manufacturing model and hired people to make the goods, but today, manufacturing is increasingly outsourced by lean organisations focused more on strategy and public relations.[16]

Surfwear company Billabong gets its edge by staying ahead of the pack, picking the trend and then outsourcing most of the production work. It's a model replicated across the economy. Biscuits and surfwear are tangible products but selling them in a highly competitive market where production is quick, cheap and easy is about coming up with a better idea and a better marketing strategy than your rival. The difference between one style of sports runner and another is largely about packaging and marketing, so competitive edge is about perception as much as reality.

Workers have experienced more and more changes in the past few years around technology and power and the move by companies to new sorts of business models. Many have crept up on us and it's a shock to discover we're suddenly conducting business over a coffee and the way we work is so different. There are paradoxes to this revolution around work. The office can still be oppressive for many people but there's been a dramatic shift in manners and individual rights. The workplace is informal enough to allow you to duck out for a coffee without feeling guilty but stress may be a routine part of your day. Employees are under more pressure to produce, yet they have more physical freedom than ever. They are constantly monitored for performance, but how they reach their targets may well be up to them. Results, dollars and the bottom line dominate their working days, yet they don't have to ask permission to go out for a cigarette. In the end, they have to sort out how to get from A to Z in their jobs, often with little help from the boss.

There's plenty of room to move within the modern workplace but that freedom is complicated. And it's not about less time or engagement on the job. Corporations demand enormous buy-in from employees in terms of values and commitment to the goals of the company. They are hooking workers into the project and the corporate way of thinking. That's no accident. It's a deliberate strategy that emerged in the 1990s as our biggest corporations faced new economic challenges.

---

1. Interview with Carl Rhodes.
2. Priest, Marcus. 'Long hours part of the job', *The Australian Financial Review*. 10 October 2003, p. 9.
3. Trinca, Helen. 'True leaders, 2002', *AFR BOSS*, Vol. 2, Number 8, August 2002, p. 51.
4. Some of the issues confronting managers of knowledge workers who surf the Net at work are examined in the following article: Oravec, Jo Ann. 'Working hard and playing hard: constructive uses of online recreation', *The Journal of General Management*. Vol. 24, Number 3, Spring 1999. An edited version was published in *AFR BOSS*. Vol. 1, Number 1. March 2000.
5. Interview with Nancy Milne.
6. Interview with John Vamos.
7. Interview with Chris Fogarty.
8. Pink, Daniel. *Free Agent Nation: The Future of Working for Yourself.* Warner Books, 2002.
9. Whyte, William H. *The Organization Man.* Jonathan Cape, 1956, p. 12.
10. Drucker, Peter. 'Beyond the information revolution, *The Atlantic Monthly*. Vol. 284, Number 4, October 1999, pp. 45–57.
11. Interview with David Rymer.
12. Trinca, Helen. 'Star system', *AFR BOSS*. Vol. 4, Number 11, November 2003, p. 62.
13. Interview with Orit Gadish.
14. Frederick Winslow Taylor (1856–1915) was an American engineer who devised one of the most influential management approaches of the 20th century. His book *The Principles of Scientific Management*, published in 1911, outlined his belief that each part of a person's work could be scientifically analysed so that managers could determine and then measure how much work he or she should do each day. An exact method could be devised for each task and this was to be followed by the workers. But it was managers, not workers, who should have the right to determine how a job

should be carried out. This approach separated the planning of work from the work itself and has been criticised as turning workers into automatons expected to simply carry out orders and who can make no contribution to the way a problem is approached.

15. Interview with Viv Read.

16. The Luken & May approach was described in *AFR BOSS*, Vol. 2, Number 2, February 2001.

2

The New Deal
of the 1990s

FLASH MOBS ARE LIKE THE Mexican Waves of the CBD. The instant mobs are summoned up via text messages on mobile phones or by email as dozens or hundreds of people converge in a public space, just because they can. When the mob forms, from Seattle to Berlin, it's making a statement about breaking free of the crowd and creating your own group event. Getting physically connected in a cyber age has never been easier. All you need is a mobile and you too can mobilise a generation. Control is no longer in the hands of a designated or elected leader or organisation. Power is in the hands of the group conjured up by modern communication. Typically, the flash mob gathers, performs a predetermined action and disperses. The phenomenon emerged strongly in 2003 with one of the best-known flash mobs gathering in an area of Grand Central Station in New York in July of that year simply to applaud loudly for fifteen seconds and then leave. Compared with an anti-war protest, flash mobs are notable for their lack of agenda. But flash mobbing is also about reacting against order and predictable structures like media, politics or the workplace. But it's not likely to change them. At the start of the 1990s it seemed like these structures were up for renegotiation. It was going to be the brave new corporate world where workers would seize the day. We've been stunned at times by the self-belief of the new generation of workers. The expectations of many young people are sky-high. 'I'd like to be considered for an editor's position,' a twenty-something applicant suggested to us once. And why not? He'd been working in the media business for a couple of years and had learnt the basics. Now it was time to make his run. In the 2002 movie *Storytelling*, written and directed by Todd Solondz, the disaffected teenage boy of a middle-class family is asked by his school counsellor about his long-term goals. The teenager says, 'I don't know . . . I just want to be on TV, maybe have a talk show.' He doesn't want to study television at college or be an apprentice. He's headed straight for the top. From zero to hero, these teenagers are volunteering for greatness. No mucking about for them – their time frame moves at SMS pace, instantaneous and growing ever faster. All around them the journey from A to B looks so quick and the results so good. They can see what the outcome of a house renovation is every night on reality TV and it all looks so easy. Why not fast-track to the top of the company?

Who can blame them for their expectations? The language of work and achievement backs them up at every turn. Corporate culture offers all of us a can-do world where anything seems possible. Popular culture reinforces the notion that the only hurdles between you and success are your own fears. Nothing a good motivational course wouldn't fix, right? An exciting, reward-ing job is everyone's birthright – all you need to know is how to compete. And then just do it, man.

Thirty years ago, when the legendary American writer Studs

Terkel set out to document work, he interviewed Americans across the country. He found them searching for 'daily meaning as well as daily bread, for recognition as well as cash, for astonishment rather than torpor; in short for a sort of life rather than a Monday through Friday sort of dying'.[1] Reading his book *Working*, published in 1972, is a shock. The words seem so out of date. It's true that modern workers want meaning, recognition and 'astonishment', or at least the contemporary version – buzz. But Terkel's depiction of Monday to Friday as the death watch is out of sync with the popular culture around work. Yes, it's tough at times, the hours are long, people bitch about the boss. But the notion that life is somewhere else and that work is the dark side is disappearing. Work is where we want to be, where many of us truly come alive, and this generation would have it no other way. Their parents yearned to drop out and join a commune, or at least freelance outside the system, but today it's different. Point me at it and tell me how to win.

How did we get here from the 1960s and 1970s, when attitudes to work and success were far more ambivalent and popular culture reinforced not the possibilities but the constraints of work? How is it that we have seemingly bought the new agenda, lock, stock and barrel?

To understand the shift, step back to the 1990s when the meaning of work was up for grabs – and the corporates seized the opportunity with both hands. This was the decade when workers were offered a new deal, one based on their becoming equal partners in the work project. It was the decade when it became acceptable for women – as well as men – to place work at the centre of life and the decade when that emphasis and dual income became an economic necessity for many. The elevation of consumption forced a strong link between work, money, buying power and status.

We've watched those changes as journalists, lived through them as workers and have recognised how powerful the new deal has been in endorsing work as a central part of modern life. At its most simplistic, the new deal offered in the 1990s was about a new way of distributing power (it's not just about the boss), a new way of running the office (dump the hierarchy), a new way of using the worker (give us your hearts, your minds, your ideas), and a new way of thinking about the company (your values are our values are your values, right?).

The shifts are not precise and the emphasis given to different elements has varied at times, but overall, in the 1990s work was repositioned as a place where the individual went for meaning. For companies, and the public sector organisations which embraced the same philosophies, the new deal delivered a workforce independent yet absolutely aligned with employers' goals. It ended the 'us and them' divide that historically had existed even in organisations without a strong adversarial or union culture. The 1990s agenda was about choices and about the possibility of having fun amid the commitment to high performance and productivity. The focus was on the employee as an individual and as a whole person whose dreams coincided happily with those of the organisation.

The language of work also changed in this period. Account executives spoke of 'emotional intelligence'; hotels relabelled their front office clerks 'managers', giving them status and responsibility, albeit on the same pay; management books urged the new 'portfolio' workers to construct careers that suited *their* lifestyle and demands. Oozing through these examples was the notion of the empowered worker who could carve his or her own path at work. Today, this rhetoric runs deep through all levels of organisations, even when the reality is far different. Words like 'values', 'alignment', 'creativity' and 'performance' are as familiar to today's corporate workers and managers as the bundy clock was to their parents. Organisations are creating a new relationship between the employee and the company using some extraordinary techniques.

Take, for example, the plastic cards, sized like credit cards, which are issued to workers at multinationals like Cisco. There's a Cisco card in our office, handed over to colleague Tony Boyd during an interview he had with John Chambers, Cisco's global CEO. Boyd, who has reported on business and finance for twenty-five years, was nonplussed when the American unhooked the card from his belt, where he always wears it, to make a point about Cisco's corporate culture. 'Changing the way we work, live, play and learn,' Chambers read from the card, giving Boyd a quick lesson in the new corporatism. According to the card, Cisco culture is about 'fun, empowerment, open communication, teamwork, continuous improvement'. It's not mandatory to wear such cards but from the late 1990s they have been routinely produced by corporations and issued as part of the initiation process of new employees. They encourage staff to get with the project. The cards, as Chambers demonstrated, are a useful ready reference, a reminder of what you're supposed to be doing at the office, something to pull out when in doubt, perhaps.[2] They are as massaged – and sometimes as banal – as the PowerPoint presentation to clients.

The first time we saw one of these cards was when John McFarlane, the chief executive of ANZ Bank, produced one from his pocket during a discussion on leadership. It was in 2001, during our magazine's selection process for a top leaders list, and McFarlane, a media-savvy and highly adept Scot, was on the panel. The card seemed almost corny then: such an item was still relatively rare in Australia. But McFarlane talked about how it carried the distilled idea of the bank's mission statement.

The statements on these cards are generally the result of a corporate culture exercise in which employees are asked to debate the values of the company and articulate its aims. Once formulated, the ideas are circulated widely through the company and the dot-point version is laminated on to employee cards. Not to be confused with the security ID card which most employees now wear around their necks or on their belts, this is a different sort of identity card, one that makes very clear an employee's identification with the company.

When CEOs like John Chambers talk about aligning the values of workers and corporations, their tone is invariably empathetic. But to many critics, there's nothing benign about this 'corporate colonisation of the self'.[3] They see it as undermining the autonomy of worker culture and creating a belief system which is heavily circumscribed and acceptable to the organisation.

Homogenising the workforce is nothing new but the 1990s push to co-opt workers at a deep emotional level grew, ironically, from the shambles of mass sackings in the previous decade.

Those were the years when the deregulation of financial systems and the free flow of capital left many big companies desperately trying to compete with cheap overseas production. The cosy protectionism of the years after the Second World War were ripped apart and companies in Australia and overseas dumped workers as they pursued their goal of remaining competitive with countries able to access a cheap labour pool. Many of the jobs lost in the First World were re-created in the Third World, but at a fraction of the cost. For those who lost their jobs and those who saw it happen, this brutal numbers game brought little credit to corporations. It was hard to trust the boss when the office seemed to be awash with pink slips announcing your colleagues' dismissals.

Employees who survived became watchful, anxious they would be next, and not necessarily persuaded to work hard for companies which seemed so heartless. It was a devastating period for many as they saw companies hollowed out, careers terminated years before retirement age and lives changed forever by a corporate sector focused on the silver bullet of 'downsizing'. The impact on individuals was intense. In the late 1990s, it was almost impossible to find senior managers prepared to go public about losing their jobs for a series in *The Sydney Morning Herald* about the massive downsizings. These men – and they were mainly men – were wary of talking about their sackings in case it harmed their chances of getting another job. The social stigma around downsizing and forced redundancies was still very high and the psychological and economic impact on people at all levels was harsh.

Yet within a few years this upheaval had been repackaged by companies, consultants, HR practitioners and governments as a way of renewing organisations, opening up jobs to competition and talent, and giving more power and responsibility to individuals. The new rhetoric was about building a different sort of organisation where employees would be in control of their own careers, free of the deadwood, free of the routine work which would now be outsourced, and free of fusty old ideas like full employment or a job for life. Plenty of room for the truly talented to emerge. Even better, workers would be treated as adults rather than children protected by a paternalistic organisation.

Corporations had little choice but to spin the dramas of the 1980s into a positive. They needed workers to stay on side. Technology made it so easy to produce cheap goods that a rival could quickly match you on price. Intellectual skills began to be highly valued as companies came to terms with living in a knowledge age. Simply being lean and mean was not enough to save your organisation: you needed the edge in ideas. What went on inside the heads of employees, even their personalities, had to be co-opted for the organisation. Companies began to think about intangible assets, like people with brains and loyalty and commitment, and how to get them to sign up to the project. It was time to think about rebuilding relationships with a workforce cynical about the actions of corporations. But what really forced the hand of the corporates was the sudden shortage of people in emerging areas – like dot coms – and bidding wars developed over high-fliers in sectors like financial services. The word was out that unless you positioned yourself as a good employer you could forget about getting the Generation X talent, precisely the group that had embraced the new technology. The old ethos of age and experience was replaced by new demands for adaptability. For corporates, the challenge was to capture people with new skills and new ideas.

At the same time, the new deal of the 1990s tapped into ideas about individuals controlling their destinies. In the twentieth century, men and women sloughed off many traditional religious and social values as their belief in human, temporal power grew. The world changed from one ordered for us by others to one which we could manage and shape. Today, many people in the West have high expectations about their rights to be happy and fulfilled and to invent themselves; to be whatever they wish to be, to create their personas along with their quasi-designer apartments. The power to create your world – largely through work and its rewards – can rival the ability of sex in providing a sense of personal power. When your identity depends less on sexual activity and more on consumption and the ability to acquire 'must have' objects, work rapidly becomes a compelling exercise. It is, after all, the path to happiness.

And unlike earlier generations who offered hard work and activity up to God, most of us expect to be happy in this world, not the next. Our demands are high and we're convinced of our right to shape our own workplaces rather than accept the patterns dictated by others. Expanded education opportunities have also raised expectations about what we want from work. In Australia, the percentage of people going to university rose significantly between 1980 and 1990. Many of this cohort were women, and the politics of feminism, as well as the simple pressure of greater numbers, forced organisations to deliver on the expectations of a highly educated and competitive workforce.

It became hard for companies to maintain the old structures. At the very least, a new language was needed to make sense of a world employees felt they could negotiate and control. Forget Organisation Man, the goal was to bring your 'real' self to work. No more role-playing or subservience to senior managers. Not only would workers all get along better and feel happier but because they were functioning as complete beings, they would deal with work issues within a holistic, ethical framework. The rhetoric for this promise often veered into self-help territory. Our emotional selves were now to be allowed into the office, where simply being smart and keeping our noses clean would no longer be enough. The idea was that shedding your work persona would bring a better outcome for all involved. But this was a promise with significant conditions attached. Companies would indeed allow us to be authentic, but only as long as our behaviour complied with the goals of the workplace. Some behaviour and emotions were acceptable and others were not.

One overt way companies could show their new colours was to allow employees to wear what they wanted to the office – on one day of the week. It might have looked like window dressing but the notion that you could break free of the suit, as well as some of the stock behaviour of Organisation Man, was hot in the 1990s. The creatives, like those who worked in the advertising industry, had always had some licence to play with corporate dress codes and wear outrageous clothing to work. Now this freedom was offered to all. Even relatively stitched-up law firms had casual Fridays when staff could wear chinos to the office. For a while, it was the big water-cooler conversation topic, more important than other issues like overtime. The fuss makes sense. Business dress carries messages about social order, hierarchy and status, and relaxing the code has an impact on all those elements. If we were indeed to become 'real people' at work, with more autonomy, surely we could choose the clothes we felt comfortable in? We could express ourselves, show our colleagues what we were like *outside* the office, assert our personal power through our clothes. What we put on every morning defines us and casual Fridays were part of a complex blending of the public and private that gathered pace in the 1990s.

Casual Fridays had little impact in some sectors, of course. Journalists, as a species, have traditionally eschewed fashion. Male journalists in the 1980s would often borrow the office tie or a colleague's jacket as they headed out to a press conference. Female journalists, with a few exceptions, tended to the neat and tidy rather than the glamorous, finished look of their contemporaries in big business or marketing. It was strange to observe what happened at the end of the 1990s in our own workplace, the Fairfax headquarters in Darling Park in Sydney. For the first time in our careers, we found ourselves sharing a floor with staff from the advertising and (for a time) marketing departments, sections of newspaper empires which had long been quarantined from the newsroom. Journalists were confronted daily (and vice versa) with a very different style of worker, who dressed very differently. The men and women of advertising and marketing were more corporate in style than journalists. And of course, it was these workers who adopted casual Fridays with alacrity.

But even something as apparently innocuous as dressing more informally seemed to run out of steam. Casual Fridays sent some professionals into a spin. They felt threatened by the idea of shedding the suit they were comfortable in and trying to work out what the new code meant. When Dr Gayle Avery, associate professor at the

Macquarie Graduate School of Management in Sydney, looked at the casual dress phenomenon around this time she found that it tinkered with a complex range of signals around status and authority.[4] Clothes carry messages about class, positioning and power, and it is not easy to dump the suit without eroding authority. Changing into jeans on Fridays sent signals that not all bosses wanted to send. Talking about empowering employees was one thing, but the new dress codes reinforced the notion that everyone was equal in the office, when clearly they were not. By the early 2000s, as the dot com boom collapsed and the brio which characterised this period disappeared, many offices quietly dispensed with the free-dress movement. The devastation of September 11, 2001, hastened the swing back to a more sombre office. The CBDs were awash with black suits again.[5]

In the 1990s, workers were given permission to at least start talking about emotions in the office. The impact of American academic and writer Daniel Goleman and others on emotional intelligence has been immense, so much so that Emotional Quotient (EQ) – which is an effort to include intuition, empathy and self-awareness in the suite of skills needed in the workplace – became almost a household phrase.[6] Through his bestselling books and seminars around the world Goleman advanced an economic argument for EQ – if you were to get workers to operate together constructively as a team in the new knowledge economy, you had to handle them differently. It was a sensible argument which corporates could embrace. But EQ also played directly to a basic need in people to be happy at work, rather than fearful. Empathy seemed like a very good idea. To be authentic at work by becoming more self-aware would be good for you and good for those in the adjoining cubicles.

Twenty years ago, the idea that you could show emotion in the office or express sadness at any real level was regarded as inappropriate. Young workers were taught by osmosis that certain issues were best left outside the office. It was considered undisciplined to bring your personal issues – a bad marriage, a sick child, an elderly parent – to the job and in many senses, it was young women, rather than young men, who were most strongly warned off. After all, they were the ones most likely to break the code of conduct in the office, weren't they? If anyone was going to introduce the personal and show emotion, it would be the women now flooding into the workplace.

For workers with pressing emotional or personal problems, or simply the day-to-day anxieties involved in running a life, the ban on being open or authentic at work was often a strain. Keeping a lid on your feelings meant developing a certain demeanour, one based on reason and logic. The workplace of the 1950s, for example, was much more likely to be about precision and replication of process than it is today. Back then, there was a kind of absolutism about work: this is how we do it. Today, business sees things differently and endorses the idea that employees can be far more useful and productive if they are allowed to exercise some of their intuitive, creative skills. EQ is far less threatening and, as Daniel Goleman has argued, can be seen as a money-making asset.

Not everyone welcomes the emotional. For some people there were advantages in shutting the personal out of the workplace. The most obvious was that when you left work you could resume your own self, be who you wanted to be without the office knowing. There was a demarcation between work and play. In a sense you could act your way through the workplace, and many of us did just that as we learnt to develop a specific persona for the office. As EQ became popular, the challenge was no longer how to switch off the personal at the beginning of the day but how to switch off *work* at the end of the day. For some people, emotional intelligence was another illustration of the personal being colonised by work. One of our colleagues surprised us one day with his anger at cultural change programs, like those introduced at

Woodside Energy in Perth or at the ANZ, which could involve workers discussing personal issues in group exercises. He could think of nothing worse than having to share personal issues in the workplace, he said. For him, having two personalities, one for work and one for home, could be tough but at least it was clear where work ended and the rest of life began.

For this person, the end of the boundary between work and life was a negative. It's understandable. If we are ourselves at work, are we supposed to be 'at work', in some senses, all the time? Is the idea of balance and some separation between work and life being lost in this rush by the company to tap into my emotional side? If I am so authentic at work, where is my protective coating when things get tough? Where is my survival kit, the mask I don for a difficult workplace? And if I am giving so much emotional, as well as intellectual and physical, energy to the company, how much is left over to invest in friendships, family, partners, and even sex? For many workers these are now rhetorical questions: the colonisation is complete, with so many spaces of our lives having already been captured by work. The emotional and intellectual grip which work has on so many of us is now a fact of life.

Our society is increasingly about a merging of public and private spaces, something which gives work a far greater power in our daily lives than ever before. Even if you opt to work outside the corporate structure as a freelancer, you may still find the balancing act between your 'real' self and your 'work' self to be tricky. Commentator Daniel Pink worries that the big attraction of freelancing, that you can integrate both sides of self, can itself be a problem. He took the freelance option a few years back and works from a room at the top of his house in Washington. On the phone to Australia one night, with his wife and kids murmuring downstairs, Pink confessed to us that work can still win, even when you think you've got a good, balanced, integrated approach.

'Because work is more deeply woven into your self, it can be harder to cast off, which means work can occasionally consume and even smother identity,' he says.[7]

This refashioning of the employee was not accidental or a natural development. At one level it was part of the spin after the 1980s downsizing. OK, if you can't trust your employer, start trusting yourself and turn a negative into a positive. The stress on the individual having a specific contract, apparently of equal power, with their employer was also a result of the growing dominance of the Right, politically, economically and culturally. Conservative political thought elevates the individual above the group or the team, and certainly above the collective activities of the union. Organised labour was a special flashpoint for conservatives, who saw unions as interfering in the direct relationships between worker and boss. A workplace conversation based around individual negotiation and power was attractive on a number of levels. By the 1990s, the Left had lost the battle for full employment as governments effectively conceded that they could not provide jobs for all their citizens. At the same time, unions failed to stem the job cuts of the 1980s and were reduced to helping sacked workers get reasonable redundancy. This was a worthy exercise but it meant that workers could no longer necessarily rely on unions to save their jobs. Companies moved quickly to exploit the loss of union power and the vulnerability of workers who had seen an end to job entitlement. The creation of the 'portfolio' worker and the contractor meant you were increasingly on your own, for better or worse.

The old contract with workers was based on payment for time on the job; now the contract could be extended to include the thinking time, the 'headspace' of workers even when they were off the job. Once the corporation made sure workers followed the rules and the processes while on the job; now it would encourage people to live and breathe their jobs. To be a good worker now required a level of engagement that earlier generations would have seen as an unhealthy addiction, as workaholism. You could still clock off at 5 p.m. and forget about work till 9 a.m. the next day but such an old-fashioned approach would see you fall behind, marginalised in a system which required a higher commitment than just being there for the formal hours of work.

Time-serving – now often labelled 'presenteeism' by management practitioners – is anathema to the modern organisation. Presenteeism is about being at the desk physically but opting out in every other way, with your heart and mind somewhere else. The disengagement of workers in a factory is dangerous – workers can be badly injured if they are on automatic pilot – but in the service and information sector the lack of involvement can be most damaging to the employer. A study released in December 2002 by the Gallup Organisation revealed that almost twenty per cent of workers in Australia are 'actively disengaged in their jobs'. They are 'psychologically absent . . . disenchanted and disaffected'.[8] These are the workers bosses fear most, not just for their loss of productive work and contribution but because they are often actively working against the cohesion and 'buy-in' of their colleagues. They are indeed the most difficult to colonise.

Another pressure on corporates during the 1990s was the search for a better balance between work and life as men and women struggled to work and raise families. The changes in women's lives which had begun in the 1960s with campaigns for equal opportunity and power in personal and professional life had, by the 1990s, made working women an entrenched part of the business world. In the period immediately after the Second World War, women had been socially engineered back to the domestic sphere after having undertaken 'war work'. Poorer women, migrants among them, continued to work in the next few decades but it would be well into the 1980s before it became routine for professional women to return to work within three or six months of giving birth. It would take another decade before women truly began to see themselves as workers first and parents second, but when that attitude began to flow through the workplace companies came under far more pressure to deliver senior jobs to women.

Surely this would be the decade when the gender divide truly disappeared, when there would be so many women around that female CEOs would no longer be a novelty? When the 'mummy track' would no longer see women excluded from top jobs? It was the decade when the debate about the glass ceiling shifted its focus from discrimination against women to discrimination against *mothers*.

As the corporates mused publicly about the long hours culture and heavy workloads and promised to look at issues like parental leave or sabbaticals, it seemed that they might indeed come up with a way for employees to combine family life with work life. There was really only one solution – to minimise hours and allow workers to carve out time for exercises like attending a mid-week sports carnival at school without feeling guilty. And the idea of balance was not just for parents: the rhetoric was that everyone would benefit if workers had a hinterland.

Far from achieving balance, the 1990s saw an increase in long hours and work at any price. It was the decade when work became more important to our society than protecting family life. The subject continued to be seen as a 'women's issue'. Men were designated primarily as workers, not parents, and the notion that any of them would have the temerity to want to see their kid's school play at 2 p.m. was alien to a corporate culture which had been formed in an age when wives stayed at home and assumed virtually all parenting duties. Those attitudes die hard. It's a shock sometimes, when so many women work, to realise that some senior corporate men have had little or no experience of working partners. When Elizabeth Proust, the most senior woman at the

ANZ Bank, looks around the table during executive management meetings she sees thirteen men, no other women, and she remembers too that she is the only one of the fourteen people there who has a working spouse.[9] Single people too, men and women, find it hard to understand just how difficult it is for parents in high-pressure workplaces. Many singles feel that they have made sacrifices, put their personal lives on hold to succeed and will not willingly make concessions to those who want both.

Our own experiences – as a single woman and one who returned to work soon after giving birth – showed us that the prevailing attitude in the 1990s was that if mothers wanted to work, whether for financial or personal reasons, let them, but there would be no changes to the structures. Workplaces remained a child-free zone and single people or those parents prepared to keep their kids out of sight and mind held the power. The promise for these workers was attractive – full-time work, long hours and total commitment would bring you a high level of success and happiness, and give purpose to your world. Part-time work was for pin money or for mothers desperate to try to keep a foot on the ladder until their kids were old enough and they could squeeze themselves back into full-time work. Maybe.

In the 1970s and 1980s, women took a few years out, and often waited until their kids went to school before returning to work. By the 1990s intense competition for jobs and the belief among women that paid work beat unpaid mothering saw many of our colleagues returning to work within months of giving birth. In the deadline zone of daily journalism, it was tough for these women. There were financial rewards, although as their wages were eaten up by childcare and nannies they wondered whether the cost–benefit ratio played out in their favour. It was tough too for their childless colleagues or the men who found themselves doing the late shifts or weekend work in an office where some staffers were suddenly on a four-day week and available only for regular daytime hours.

The 1990s was the decade when it became clear that work would continue to take up a big slice of our time. As the work portion increased, the time available for the personal was reduced. It wasn't exactly work as the new sex, but the time pressures on many people saw them juggling relationships as they once juggled visits to the hairdresser or a round of golf. And the absorbing nature of work has a practical rationale: who of us now really believes that we will easily retire at the age of fifty-five or sixty, or even sixty-five? In our areas of media and information, we assume we will keep working, in one way or another, for many years – largely because we will have to if we want to maintain a good standard of living. It's perhaps not surprising that work is so engrossing. Employees need to learn how to love it if they are to keep going long enough to fund an extended older age. It's a conundrum for many: you work hard to maintain a lifestyle and then find there is little time to enjoy it. Yet, increasingly, the enjoyment may come from the power your work gives you to acquire consumer goods.

There was a period in the 1990s when the dot com boom seemed to promise a very different style of working. Dot coms were about speed and surprise, about being able to work in unconventional ways in unconventional settings. These businesses pushed the boundaries of technology and the way services were created and provided. Working on the Web could mean working from home or working from Hawaii. It was a heady period when MBAs and McKinsey consultants grabbed their chances and launched into start-up mode. It seemed a long way from traditional work.

Technology seemed to hold out the chance for employees to have a truly mobile working life. Not just telecommuting from home for one employer, although that became viable for some workers quite quickly. The other option was working from a café, a client's office – away from base. Of course, mobility meant a higher level of trust too, a part of the new work contract that made many employers distinctly uncomfortable. Employees too were hesitant about the options technology brought. Telecommuting could mean isolation, procrastination, even boredom, and for workaholics there was no true end to the working day. The promise was to have the freedom to work in your own environment, but what then of the social aspects of the office? And what would it do to career prospects? And who would monitor the workers?

Supervision has always been an issue for companies. But the new deal suggested that there could be new ways of controlling your staff, although the C-word was not to be used. The old systems of clocking on and off work or of supervisors managing lunchbreaks and activity levels were increasingly hard to maintain. And anyway, attendance was only the first step at workplaces where mental and emotional engagement had become so important. No longer able to demand productivity, companies sought alternative methods of ensuring workers gave one hundred per cent at the office. Fear of sacking, or ambitions for career advancement, would ensure that some employees worked hard, but the promise of the 1990s went far beyond that to the idea that workers who adopted the company's goals as their own would give everything to the project.

It was a period when companies began seeking outside help to shift the attitudes of workers. Management consultants and human resource specialists encouraged companies to use their services for seminars or other interactive exercises in the workplace in order to create mission statements and lists of values and objectives. The overt message was that workers could influence the direction of the company. The reality was often that unless workers 'came on board' and embraced the project, they could miss out on promotions and success.

In short, companies looked for an intense sense of ownership in their employees, an ownership based on emotion, not dollars. There was a new exchange being promoted, one in which freedom to be yourself at work was offered as the replacement for lost security and faded loyalties. Employment was far less certain, but for those savvy enough to have a job, work would be a lot more interesting and much more fun.

That was the promise. The reality was that by the end of the 1990s, the economy was off the boil after the enthusiasm of a bull market and the magic of the Internet. The possibility of a different kind of workplace seemed to evaporate. The buoyancy and euphoria of the 1990s collapsed. The new economy didn't arrive. But many people were already beginning to find new reasons to feed their obsession with jobs and keep working harder.

1. Terkel, Studs. *Working*. The New Press, 1972, p. xi.
2. Boyd, Tony. 'Wonder boy', *AFR BOSS*. Vol. 3, Number 4, April 2002, pp. 18–22.
3. Aldridge, Alan. *Consumption*. Polity, 2002, p. 46.
4. Interview with Dr Gayle Avery.
5. In February 2004, David Murray, the CEO of the Commonwealth Bank, told a Sydney lunch that he did not think employees should don casual gear, stating '[I] fundamentally hate mufti.' (Reported in *The Sydney Morning Herald*, 18 February 2004, p. 23.) A survey released that month by the recruitment firm Talent 2 said that only 28.7 per cent of Australian companies still allowed their employees to wear casual dress on Fridays.
6. Daniel Goleman's ideas on Emotional Intelligence have been detailed in several books and articles, including *Emotional Intelligence: Why it Can Matter More Than IQ*. Bloomsbury, 1998.
7. Interview with Daniel Pink.
8. The *Australian Engagement Study* was conducted by Gallup in September/October 2002 using a sample of 1000 working Australians aged 18 and over.
9. Elizabeth Proust told this story during a Sydney lunch address in November 2003.

3

God to the gold card: what drives us to work

CELEBRITY CHEFS LIKE NIGELLA LAWSON and Jamie Oliver are powerful actors in a drama many of us play out daily – shopping. These television cooks can literally move a product if they mention it on their shows. The conventional wisdom is that Nigella 'made' the mezzaluna, the half-moon shaped Italian knife which now seems mandatory for Australian foodies. Jamie did much the same for the mortar and pestle when he started grinding away during his appearances on the box. Our enthusiasm for these relatively cheap items is just one symptom of our enthusiasm for consumption. We're all shoppers now, flocking to malls, boutiques and discount retailers in search of things to have and to hold. And if we can't get out there among it, there's always the Internet or, better still, the Shopping Channel.

Once we were restricted to shopping at certain hours, rarely if ever on Sundays, and the choice of product was limited. Shopping was a process, not an end in itself. While there have always been those rusted-on shoppers among us – people who are happiest snooping for bargains and quality and rare items and for whom queues and delays and unhelpful sales people are simply Everests to be conquered – this species has multiplied dramatically. We're all shopping more and apparently we're loving it.

It seems that buying carries a pleasure quite separate from ownership of the product itself. At the giant malls on the outskirts of our cities or in CBD department stores, shopping is often a leisure activity, with the precinct a place to take the whole family for a day out. For some it's retail therapy, the reward for a rough day at the office and a release from the stress and straitjacket of work. At another level, shopping hard is also about our search for meaning and it subtly locks us into what American economist and author of *The Overworked American*, Juliet Schor, terms the 'work-and-spend cycle'.[1] Increasingly, many of us have many possessions in our lives and we buy more and more. We may not need these goods but we want them – and we're buying largely because we can. We have enormous choice in consumer products, many of which are substantially cheaper than ever before, thanks to Third World labour, technology and oversupply. Modern marketing turns products into dreams that are buyable and dreams into products we can purchase. What we buy helps define us to others and to ourselves. Once we were producers of goods – the home-cooked meal or the furniture made in the factory – but no longer. For many of us, our primary sense of self comes from what we purchase, whether it be the new sofa or the original artwork.

People have been aided and abetted in this by a massive expansion in available and relatively cheap credit which has fuelled a consumption-driven recovery in the West. In Australia, household debt (money borrowed against the house or on credit cards) is higher than ever. Again it's the market at work. Over-capacity throughout the Western world has meant that the only way the system can keep ticking over is for consumers to keep on shopping. In many sectors we are simply producing far more than we could ever sell without the assistance of a consumer culture – a culture largely defined by what it consumes, rather than by what it creates, bolstered by easy access to credit.

As our purchases have increased, so has the role given to consumption in our culture. While the term 'consumption' once referred to the food we ate or the wine we drank, it is now applied to every aspect of our lives. Even our children can be seen as objects of emotional consumption, wanted for the joy they can bring.[2] Other sorts of relationships are increasingly defined in terms of what they can give us, of what we can enjoy or gain from the other person. They must deliver something to us or they are discarded. We befriend people but expect them to deliver us jobs, contacts or sales leads. In our intimate relationships we demand that *our* needs are met, in language that did not exist fifty years ago.

Today, some form of consumption, either of goods or experience, is a reason for being, and therefore a reason for being at work. But consumption plays a dual role: it helps drive us to work and it sits alongside work as a way of defining us. Work delivers status and a public demonstration of where we sit in the pecking order. Sometimes the ground rules shift about which jobs carry the most prestige: today's hot job was a non-event a decade ago. Just think of the low status of cooking and catering jobs in the 1970s compared with the way every teenager now wants to be a chef. We've traditionally slotted people into social hierarchies based on their paid work, but now it's not the only benchmark. The rewards of work – the holidays at the snow, the Alessi kettle, the harbour-side house, the tickets to the rugby – help us position ourselves in our various communities. These are things we can purchase but they describe who we are, to ourselves and to others.

Consumption extends to the services people use to have their houses cleaned, gardens maintained and dogs walked. You pay for these relatively humdrum chores to be done by others so that you have time to relax, go to the gym or focus on your children. The personal is outsourced, as highly organised as your working life. There is even a certain kudos in having your shirts laundered and ironed or your dinner cooked by the housekeeper.

Highly sought-after objects like gold, silver and horses have always defined their owners but we have now broadened the range of goods by which we are judged. Products of all sorts and prices carry meaning and bestow value on their owners. We lust after designer goods as deeply as we lust after the good-looking designer: who needs sex when you can get off on acquiring the latest Gucci bag?

It's stunning to see the popularity of reality television shows like *Backyard Blitz*, which carry the promise of instant style and reinvention. There's a level of decorator porn in these shows but the magic is the ease of remaking a house and, by extension, a life. The influence of these shows on what we consume is high – the renovation team determines the look and the populace follows. Even more culturally interesting is the American television show *Queer Eye for the Straight Guy*, where five gay men, style queens from Manhattan, do an instant makeover on a straight man who is invariably struggling not just with his look, but with his romantic relationship. Enter the 'Fab Five' to recast the guy's home, style and sex life. The link between consumer items, self-image and happiness is complete. Get the right shirt and you get the girl. Viewers may cringe at the aesthetic or lament the way bedrooms and bathrooms across Western democracies are all beginning to look the same, but there is no denying the power of consumer items in our culture.

Queer Eye suggests that anyone can buy a lifestyle. And why not? After all, when companies can produce items incredibly cheaply in countries like China; when they can build mega-markets through free television exposure or even through word-of-mouth; when high design filters down to the low-cost Philippe Starck range at Target, then it is clear that you don't need a lot of money to be part of consumer society. You just need some. And you have to shop.

There is little escape from this cycle of work and spend. As journalists, we've been intrigued by a recent website called Radar, developed by colleagues at the Fairfax-owned newspaper *The Sydney Morning Herald*. Radar complements a weekly section of the same name in the *Herald*, which is focused on the intersection between work and play that now describes the world of the modern worker. Consumption plays a big part – especially on the website. Each week you can log in and vote for or against the choices of clothing made by lucky punters given $200 to buy a wardrobe. What we found so interesting about this interactive exercise was its sharp appreciation of the times and the enthusiasm for shopping – and Radar's ability to make the link back to the workplace. Once again, the circle of work, life and consumption is reinforced. Once it would have seemed frivolous to link the employment section of a newspaper with consumption but Radar makes the connection seamlessly. In fact, Radar replaced a mid-week Careers section and the change was driven by the paper's belief that to offer readers a section on work, separated from the rest of their lives, is outdated.

American novelist Chuck Palahniuk is another who has nailed the culture, although he's set himself up as critic rather than as a player in the rush to consume. In his anarchic novel *Fight Club*, written in 1996 and later made into a film starring Brad Pitt, a character remarks: 'You have a class of young strong men and women, and they want to give their lives to something. Advertising has these people chasing cars and clothes they don't need.

Generations have been working in jobs they hate, so that they can buy what they don't really need.'[3]

Palahniuk's take is a relatively conventional view: that people are manipulated by capitalism and big companies into spending their dollars to keep the system going. At the other end of the spectrum sits Virginia Postrel, a former editor of *Reason* magazine and a widely published columnist and author. In her 2003 book, *The Substance of Style: How the Rise of Aesthetic Value is Remaking Commerce, Culture, and Consciousness*, she argues that our focus on designer goods and appearances is a positive part of human progress. Her 'age of look and feel' does not stem from an economic system that forces 'young strong men and women' into shopping malls when they should be out reforming the system. Rather, she argues, a free market system has allowed people the freedom to buy and create themselves.[4]

For many of us, buying the goods and services we want does wonders psychologically. When we spend, we see the rewards of our hard work. Once those rewards were more abstract. We may have felt happy that we were doing our duty to God or our community, or enjoyed the feeling that work was itself a virtuous activity, a good thing to do. Our reward for work was financial but also spiritual or religious. Materialism, hedonism, the linking of happiness with consumption were all regarded as dubious pursuits in a religious age, but for our secular world there is no shame in being shallow enough to lust after a mezzaluna or a mortar and pestle. Consumption has filled a vacuum of meaning in the twenty-first century and plays a powerful role in our ambitions. You may not get an interesting job – after all, not everyone can – but you can moderate the anger and sadness at missing out by buying hard, by acquiring goods that describe you and how you live your life.

This has been a big cultural shift, one which we have seen in our own lifetimes. We each had parents who had lived through the Second World War and a period of relative austerity. The houses we grew up in were comfortable but, by today's standards, empty of product. We were surrounded by far less furniture and far fewer objects, appliances, toys and kitchen machines and utensils. About the only area where we outdid many of today's homes was in books, of which there were as many as our parents could afford. It was simply harder to obtain so much stuff, even in the 1970s. It's a different story today.

According to sociologist Alan Aldridge, 'consumer goods are ideally fitted to the modern project of identity because they can so easily be obtained, consumed and discarded.'[5] Corporations are a powerful part of all this: they not only dispense the jobs, they have a big vested interest in their workers shopping as hard as they work. Capitalism depends on production and consumption being aligned with each other.

So modern workers have become consumers par excellence, not just of goods but of experiences which are streamlined to fit their packed timetables. Employees may be working longer, but the idea of play, of entertainment, of peak experiences centred around food, wine, sport and the arts, is intense. OK, so you take the ten-day break to an exotic location, rather than the month-long holiday; you cram in drinks, a movie, then dinner on a Saturday evening when once just one of those events would have been the prime social activity for the weekend. You can have it all, even with less time to spare.

Few of us would see ourselves just working for money, even though we know we can't survive and protect and provide for our families without dollars. Work is a far more complex undertaking and even in a secular age it remains a blend of the social, the material and the spiritual. Work is the given and it is hard to imagine not working at least some of the time. If you decide not to work you risk not only poverty but exclusion. Without a job it is hard to slot into the world. You are easily ignored and virtually invisible. On the other hand, work locks you into a world of belonging and, if you choose, a world of houses, families and children. If you want these things, you will have to work. And our lives must fit around work, not the reverse – work becomes a base from which to negotiate a place in the community.

Academic Sharon Beder, who has written extensively about the 'spin' that has been used by churches, corporations, political leaders and commentators to build the work ethic, says work is so deeply ingrained in workers at all levels that 'no matter how uncomfortable it gets, they can't imagine anything else. The more hours you work, the less time you have to sit back and think about alternatives, you don't even bother to try to think of them.'[6] Beder, a professor at Wollongong University who has decamped to the south coast of New South Wales to churn out a range of books, admits she suffers from a strong work ethic. So she runs an interesting race: simultaneously critiquing the powers that have embedded paid work and success so deeply into the culture and gaining immense satisfaction from hard work and achievement. It's a paradox that many of us face. We can see the forces lined up against us and the extent to which we are psychologically and emotionally manipulated to work hard while at the same time getting a kick out of our own work.

Then again, anyone working today comes to the job with a few centuries of conditioning about the inevitability of work and its intrinsic value. The Protestant work ethic still helps determine how most of us think about work, and shapes public policy in areas like unemployment benefits, where payments are seen as a gift rather than a right. We don't talk about religion and morality so much these days but they still play a part in why people work the way they do. Deeply held ideas about industriousness and its

link to redemption – if not now, at least in the afterlife – are close
to the surface in any examination of why we work.

God was co-opted early in the industrial age to deliver disciplined, acquiescent workers to the booming factories and mills.
Centuries earlier, people like St Augustine had talked about good
works as an offering to God. But in the industrial age, it was the
paid work of the new workplaces which was invested with value
above mere wages or profits. The factory owners could not cope
with workers, like those who tended the fields, who downed tools
when they had made enough money to eat for the day. Factories
were designed to run for long hours, producing goods for sale and
they needed workers who were regimented enough to turn up and
keep turning up. As Beder shows in her 2000 book *Selling the
Work Ethic: from Puritan Pulpit to Corporate PR*, the system needed
workers who would stick at the task because it was their duty to
God and to the society which regulated behaviour. There were
limited financial rewards and much exhaustion and exploitation in
the mills, but if you submitted to the discipline of industrialised
production, you would be sure to get your reward in the next life.

Just as it is today, a key requirement for industry was a pool of
disciplined workers. An industrial age needed employees able to fit
into the rhythm of the factory. It's taken for granted now that most
work takes place in structured workplaces, with people arriving at
regular times to work for at least eight hours every day. The individual's personal rhythms are out of place in most working
environments: it is the rhythm of the office or organisation which
sets the pace and the rules. It doesn't matter that there are some
times of the day or some periods when we can't really operate
effectively, when our body clocks fail us – the pressure of centuries
keeps every generation in check. But that control was hard won
and factory owners at times needed God's help to achieve it.
Sharon Beder notes that in the nineteenth century the Methodist

Church was called upon to reinforce the godliness of work to a whole class of factory workers. The Church taught submission to authority along with thrift and the need to take individual responsibility for success. It also taught resignation to the existing social order. What a gift to wealthy capitalists who suffered no dissent from workers, even if they were wretchedly poor or exploited!

'There is some debate about which came first, the Protestant ethic or the beginnings of modern capitalism,' writes Beder. 'But one doesn't need to prove a causal relationship between one and the other to argue that the Reformation provided moral support and legitimacy to a class of people who had an interest in raising the status and influence of commerce and industry . . . Protestantism provided a conducive environment for capitalism to flourish in and the moral high ground from which to pursue profit freely and with good conscience.'[7]

God had been good for capitalism but so too was another idea that emerged in the nineteenth and early twentieth centuries – that the individual could create his or her own success. All that was needed was hard work and application, and you too could get to be President of the United States of America, or at least you would rise on your merits. Sharon Beder argues that even though the self-made man was the exception not the rule in the United States, the myth was promoted endlessly in books and children's stories because it gave workers another reason to work. Those who worked would be rewarded with better jobs and upward economic mobility – in other words, they would get their just deserts. Today, even as it is patently clear that our success in life is determined to some extent by accidents, like being born in Australia rather than Africa, we are encouraged to believe that our rewards are a result of our willingness to work hard.

Industrial-age workers were heavily controlled and supervised as they bent themselves to doing God's will and working hard. But over time, workers have so internalised the values of the workplace that voluntary compliance has become a key part of the way we work. The move to encourage workers to identify with their work so that they discipline and supervise themselves took off mid-way through the twentieth century and has been a remarkable achievement by capitalism which 'demands that workers internalise the corporate culture unquestioningly,' according to Alan Aldridge.[8]

This inner clock has long been a part of the professionals' code – the doctor, the lawyer, even the journalist, has been bred on the notion that his or her first responsibility is to the profession and/or their clients. Self-regulation means self-supervision. But in recent decades, workers at all levels have been encouraged to take more responsibility for the success of the company. One way is through workers being offered a share of profits – either through a collective agreement or more commonly through individual contracts. In other, less tangible ways, too, workers are invited to take the company's problems on board. Corporate values have been sold very successfully to communities, thanks to company public relations and advertising campaigns, and internal cultural change programs. The company PR effort is not new. Sharon Beder found that even in 1950 there were 6,500 company magazines in the United States, distributed to eighty million employees. By 1955, more than eighty per cent of firms were writing letters to individual employees on particular issues. 'The aim of all this literature was to promote a sense of purpose in the worker's job, a feeling of pride in the company they worked for, a feeling of participation in the whole enterprise, a closer relationship with management and a sense of having shared goals.'[9] This process continues today in the overt effort by companies to align the attitudes and values of staff with the values of the company. There's nothing necessarily malevolent about this exercise, and although it often lacks transparency, it creates a conforming, more manageable workforce. At a broader social level, the acceptance of corporate values in the past fifty years, especially in the past decade or so, has meant that our identities are increasingly tied to our jobs.

Where once sexual attraction and relationships drove humans, many now define themselves through work. From work comes money and the capacity to live and enjoy consumer items but also status, affirmation and self-definition, especially if you are winning inside the system. This means too that work plays a part in defining our private lives. Many people meet their life partners in the office or through work-related networks, such as those that form at the pub after hours. This seems particularly the case in the decades since women entered the workforce: who needs the tennis club when the sexes share the same desk? Sexual games in the office are now outlawed by legislation but that doesn't stop the connections being made. Even after partnerships have sorted, unsorted and re-sorted, there is a level of social–sexual engagement in offices that brings a certain frisson, and at times a messy distraction, to the workplace. The other side of our lives intrudes into working hours, despite the overt and covert sanctions that companies try to impose. Even so, ambition and the pressure to commit to work tend to have a flattening effect on the libido. The thrusting young things recognise quickly that getting ahead can often require an end to flirtation and a single-minded focus on more serious matters. Survival of the species may long have been about sex but survival for corporate man or woman is about work, to the exclusion, if necessary, of everything else.

But sexual or otherwise, work is hugely affirming to many of us. And this is not surprising, given the decline of religion, community, political parties, even true national belonging. Other than sport – and in a country like Australia, sport plays a big role in identity – what can possibly compete with work as a means of earning status and acceptance? Little wonder that employees increasingly self-monitor and self-discipline. Success in the work project is as important to them as it is to the boss. They have a lot to gain from internalising a strong work ethic.

John McGrath, the Sydney real estate executive who has had great success in his sector in recent years, is single-minded. In 2003 he told a reporter that he never sleeps past dawn: 'If you're an avid, excited entrepreneur – an adventurer in the world of business – you don't have to force yourself to get up in the morning. I just can't wait to get into work!'[10]

Outside of this work ethic, support from lovers, families and friends is still important but those relationships are now fitted in around work, changing their nature and intensity. We deal with them in short grabs and we demand of them some of the same qualities we demand of our work: flexibility, fluidity and the opportunity to change.

Listen to the words of scholar Zygmunt Bauman when he talks about his notion of 'liquid love' – the love we have now which is based largely on a fluid approach to our lives and relationships. People, he writes, now tend to speak of networks rather than partners: '"Network" suggests moments of "being in touch" interspersed with periods of free roaming . . . A twenty-eight-year-old man from Bath, interviewed in connection with the rapidly growing popularity of computer dating at the expense of singles bars and lonely-heart columns, pointed to one decisive advantage of electronic relations: "you can always press delete".'[11]

Sociologist Barbara Pocock found women and men groaning under the weight of too much to do in too little time: 'There's no space or energy left for social or community activities; no time to care for themselves or their families. Work has entered into intimate relationships too – friendships are jettisoned because they take up precious hours.'[12]

In the past decade, we have seen work invade the space once

filled by other institutions like religion and family. These personal areas have been condensed in terms of the time and energy people are prepared to spend on them. But it would be wrong to suggest that everyone is angry or oppressed by the long-hours culture at work or the way they are encouraged to spend time away from the office thinking about their next PowerPoint presentation. The central thesis of this book is that many people are consumed by work because it is the element of their lives which is most affirming.

Once the stay-at-home wife and mother had a prime role in affirming husband and children. But women are no longer so available for this task, now that they too are getting satisfaction at work. Men, unaccustomed over generations to playing such a support role, have not, so far, filled the void, in part because the structure of their jobs blocks any real possibility of change in their personal lives. For many men and women, the level of affirmation they receive from work removes the need for fulfilling partnerships outside. The flip side is that some people wind up without the partnership and without the affirmation: their struggle to survive at work saps them of the energy needed for intimacy without delivering real emotional rewards.

One of the few sources of meaning outside work is sport. Not necessarily playing it but certainly following it on television or at the game. This interest in sport and identification with Australia's national team or local competitions has increased in the past ten or fifteen years. Sport, traditionally of considerable interest to Australians, has been shanghaied by politicians in the service of nationalism and by business in the service of commerce. In the process, Australians increasingly use spectator sports to unwind from the tensions of the office and to engage with something other than work. Cultural theorists have always had a field day with sport, arguing that it has replaced religion, family and community. But the commercialisation of sport, the expansion of codes and sports across national borders (baseball anyone?) thanks to pay television, means that we are now able to watch more sport than ever before. Whether it is providing real meaning or simply filling up the hours previously spent watching black and white movies on television is a moot point. What corporations find in sport is a channel to reach a mass audience and a popular way to entertain clients and to network. Corporate sport is not just about the golf game any more – an exercise which is no longer practical for many executives because of time pressures and because it also tends to exclude women. Rather, corporate sport is likely to be about the invitation to a football or cricket game, the tennis or even swimming trials.

The corporate world also uses sport to fudge the line between work and life. The link is quite conscious and overt: the personal is brought into work in the same way that work invades personal space through modern communications. It's a perfect circle.

As work continues to take up more time, you fit your life around it. Out in the suburbs, it's really only the kids who are playing sport, as parents take on the role of chauffeur to get them to Saturday games and training. Who has time for a local team when so much of the day is taken up with work? Even here, the job dictates the kinds of physical activity that many employees pursue. Professionals are knocking on the door of expensive gymnasiums at 5.30 a.m., desperate to fit in their workouts before their 7 a.m. start at the office. Some will pound the pavements, while a lucky few will find enough time to play touch football – at lunchtime. Some bosses will encourage staff to take part in the corporate fun runs now a regular event in many cities. The annual JP Morgan Chase Corporate Challenge series is now a worldwide event. The Sydney race, around Centennial Park in Sydney at 6 p.m. on a balmy November night, now attracts more than 5,000 competitors who race individually or in teams based on their companies. There's corporate hospitality and beer tents for the runners but for most competitors this event appears to be a deadly serious competition, rather than a social night. They're applying the same intensity to the race as to any other exercise in the office. They are working hard at every aspect of corporate existence.

Working hard is easy when it all goes to plan and you feel fulfilled, empowered and in control, but what happens when work fails to measure up and fulfil your needs? Despite the problems, the resilience of the work ethic in our culture is apparent when work itself fails to deliver, and yet people stick to the script. In an economic recession or downturn, for example, the work ethic is quickly reinvented to accommodate a reality that on the surface doesn't seem to add up. One such crunch time was in the 1980s when corporations around the world dramatically sacked workers as they re-engineered their organisations in order to cut costs. To lose a job for incompetent or inadequate performance is one thing; to lose it because there are not enough jobs around is quite another. Worse still when there seems no real reason for a sacking other than the quest for a higher share price. What is surprising is that workers have by and large accepted these decisions easily, despite the fact that redundancies, at least officially, have nothing to do with an individual's performance. Workers who lose their jobs often blame themselves, not the company.

At a political level, the past twenty years have seen a major change in the way governments sell the employment issue to the electorate. Once it was up to the government to put in place the conditions where jobs could be created, if not create some of its own in the public sector, but since the 1980s governments around the world have thrown up their hands and announced it is all too hard. Nothing they can do. Globalisation wrecked the chances of a national government being able to intervene to ensure jobs for its people. By the end of the 1990s, the message had become even more acute – the real blame for unemployment lay at the feet of individuals. To work was to be part of society. Any job, no matter how banal or poorly paid, was an entree to that society. Politicians, business people and media commentators reinforced the idea that good jobs are won through merit and application. Essentially, those in work were invited to see themselves as somehow better than those who had missed out. And those out of work were invited to see themselves as failures who either were not smart enough to get a job or who were clearly too lazy to work. This is sometimes true but such an analysis ignores more complex social and economic issues.

This has left most people with little choice but to absorb the prevailing attitudes towards work and move on. Work *is* an entree to a wider and more welcoming society. Extended unemployment is destructive not only economically but psychologically. If our culture encourages us to find meaning and purpose in work, it's not surprising that unemployment can leave us disoriented. Where will we find meaning if we are unable to work? Given the strength of political and corporate power, it is not surprising that we have accepted, almost without a whimper, the way it dominates the culture. Anyway, our love affair with work goes right back to that Protestant work ethic which saw an absolute value in work itself.

When film director Baz Luhrmann says that 'work is the prayer', as he did in an interview for *The Australian Magazine* in 2003, it's startling. In a secular age, we don't expect mention of the spiritual or a direct connection between God and work to be articulated by someone as cool as Baz.[13] Yet Luhrmann, who has made movies like *Strictly Ballroom* and *Moulin Rouge*, is making a big claim for his work, linking it with an abstract search for meaning, placing it on a level beyond mere commerce. Such a link draws on centuries of cultural conditioning. Not many of us today would join with Luhrmann in seeing work as a prayer, but we want our work to have an impact, to make a difference. We look to work to provide purpose. We may not see work as having a spiritual dimension yet we want it to answer some of the deeper questions about the meaning of our lives.

Despite the anger and cynicism many employees may feel about their organisations, there is a desire to see work as an authentic part of their lives. It is not work that is the problem but those who seek to dictate the way we should operate at work.

For some of us, the love affair with work has morphed into a kind of addiction which, like other addictions to drugs or alcohol, fills the void. And like drugs or alcohol, work can be an end in itself, a way to obtain a buzz, an adrenaline rush of control and power, however short-lived. For many people, the escape into work, away from other pressing realities like family, is like the escape offered by drugs or alcohol. When Jean-Yves, one of the characters in French writer Michel Houellebecq's novel *Platform*, is described as working 'because he had a taste for work', he's talking about a sort of addiction, or at least a great pleasure.[14] Jean-Yves is a young Parisian on the way up in his travel company, working very hard as he puts the office ahead of family and personal relationships. But his intense performance is not based on any idealistic notion that his job will make a difference: he's not trying to save the world. Nor is he motivated by money. Rather, Jean-Yves is a kind of addict who works because he wants it. It is a drug, Houellebecq seems to be saying, as mood altering and energising as any other. Once a whole generation gets hooked, look out. Work can be as destructive to personal relationships, intimacy and sex as alcohol or heroin.

1. Schor, Juliet. *The Overworked American: The Unexpected Decline of Leisure.* Basic Books, 1992, p. 112.
2. Bauman, Zygmunt. *Liquid Love.* Polity, 2003, p. 42.
3. Palahniuk, Chuck. *Fight Club.* W.W. Norton & Company, 1996, p. 149.
4. Virgina Postrel, *The Substance of Style: How the Rise of Aesthetic Value is Remaking Commerce, Culture, and Consciousness.* HarperCollins, 2003.
5. Aldridge, op cit., p. 29.
6. Much of the thinking in this chapter flowed from an interview with Sharon Beder in December 2002 and from reading her book *Selling the Work Ethic: From Puritan Pulpit to Corporate PR.* Scribe Publications, 2000.
7. Ibid, p. 26.
8. Aldridge, op cit., p. 45.
9. Beder, op cit., p. 117.
10. Cadzow, Jane. 'Position, position, position', *The Good Weekend.* 1 November 2003, p. 22.
11. Bauman, op cit., p. xii.
12. Pocock, Barbara. *The Work/Life Collision.* Federation Press, 2003, p. 167.
13. Lahr, John. 'Strictly Luhrmann', *The Australian Magazine.* 1 March 2003, p. 14.
14. Houellebecq, Michel. *Platform.* William Heinemann, 1999, p. 308.

4

Collective power: unions to HR

I$^{\text{T'S A BALMY}}$ S$_{\text{YDNEY NIGHT AND MORE}}$ than 300 people – chief executives, Human Resources directors, marketing managers and PR directors – have gathered at the Art Gallery of New South Wales for a ceremony to honour the nation's best employers.[1] The winners are announced and the CEOs move to the stage to collect their trophies amid shouts of glee and applause from their colleagues. Being named as a good employer is fun but it's also worthwhile. The winning companies, judged on their policies and feedback from employees, will use the 'Best Employer' tag in their promotions and recruitment drives and to motivate staff. Not that their staff need much motivating – a company must have a positive response from workers to get on the list. If you want to make the cut for Best Employer make sure your workers are on board with the project.

Later, as the drinks flow, a manager from one of Australia's leading companies tells us that the top five companies on the list have relatively weak union cultures or are union-free. His company, he says, would be up there with the best except that half of its employees belong to a strong union. If his company wants to win it will have to do more to engage this group because right now these unionised employees are diffident towards the company and, he suspects, prosaic about the way they answer any survey on good bosses.

'These guys earn good money, they've worked in the company for years, they know they've got great jobs and their friends know they have got great jobs,' he says. 'But there's no way they will give the company credit for that.'

He is not being critical of unions or of his employees. It's just that in a strong union culture, even a good boss is not going to win many plaudits. The companies at the top of the Best Employer list, which include the travel agency Flight Centre and the multi-national IT company Cisco, get there, this manager believes, because their employees are happy to endorse their management and programs. Neither of them, nor the other winners on that night – Virgin Blue, Seek Communications and Diageo Australia – have strong union cultures (although that may change at Virgin Blue where unions have recruited recently). In companies with a strong union presence, there will be far more reservation about helping the boss win a Best Employer's Logie.

This take on events illustrates some of the tensions between unions and the HR departments of our big companies. The Best Employers list sits very comfortably in the Human Resources movement – HR – not the rather less fashionable idea of industrial relations – IR. This competition draws on the idea of empowerment and partnership at work, where the boss provides not just good wages and conditions, but offers promotional pathways and promotes good work/life balance.

Unions draw on a different story, one in which the boss must often be dragged screaming to the compromises forced by workers, and where the boss is often your enemy and rarely your buddy. It's no news that unions have struggled to hold on to members for the past couple of decades. Unions now cover only 23.1 per cent of Australian workers, a dramatic fall from the peak years – more than fifty per cent of employees were union members in 1976.[2] No news either that beating back the unions has allowed some employers to cut conditions, employ far more casual workers and control wages. But just as interesting is the way that weaker unions have opened up the space for employers to develop a new story around work.

When Patrick boss Chris Corrigan took on the maritime union in the 1998 docks dispute, he also unlocked attitudes among some Australians that had seemed dormant – strong support for the idea of workers joining together to protect their patch. But it seemed like the last hurrah. Corporations have stolen emotional ground from the unions and filled it with a different story about work, one that is viewed warily by unions and their members. It's tricky convincing workers to adopt the values of the company, but the weakening of unions has made it that much easier. Companies can only compete for the hearts and minds of workers when unions have little leverage.

Traditionally, unions have depicted workers as suffering at the hands of the system. Here is a man (or sometimes a woman) whose potential to be fully human is blocked by the work offered to him or her by the company. The worker's real life begins when he leaves the factory gate and returns to family, to community. 'Workers would down tools and go to the Mechanics Institute, not just to read Marx but to read Carlyle and Dickens,' says cultural theorist Meaghan Morris.[3] Capitalism was a scarifying experience but learning could heal the pain. The union was your protector and could demand your loyalty. Union leaders were often the mediators between the worker and the boss.

David Harman, a Canberra consultant who first went to work in Britain in the 1950s, remembers being surprised at what he found there. He'd been reared in a socialist, working-class family by a father who was an active union member. At the printing plant, Harman realised it was the union that ran the place. The foremen and supervisors left it to the senior people in the union to decide who would work and how. It was the union leader who dealt directly with the bosses. A similar system operated at Australian ports for decades, leaving some bosses at Chris Corrigan's stevedoring company lamenting that they often could not deal directly with employees. Breaking the union grip on the wharves during the 1998 docks strike was in part about sorting out a culture where the 'third force' of the union intervened between employee and employer.

At its bluntest, union activity at this time cast the employer as the enemy and the union as the saviour. Unions were the buffers between workers and employers. The worker was by definition honest and potentially heroic. Work was essential for survival and to maintain your role in the larger community. It was important to work hard and fairly. But work could be snatched from you, destroying your family and your world. Your only protection was to join the community of workers because no matter how reasonable the boss, at the end of the day he or she could not be trusted.

This adversarial culture has been very strong in some sectors of the Australian workforce, such as the construction industry. Other workplaces, like our own, have seen a milder version of unions versus boss. As journalists, writing in the area of management, we have sometimes been surprised at the suspicion towards any idea promulgated by management or the HR department. A healthy scepticism we could understand, but at times there has been a knee-jerk reaction against any effort to bring managerial practices to the newsroom. The introduction of performance reviews, taken for granted in other sectors, was initially derided by some journalists who argued strongly that they were professionals whose work could not be judged against precise performance indicators. Performance reviews may indeed be poorly executed at times or too prescriptive at others, but not every management idea is wrong. And let us not forget that the media itself has often argued for people like public servants to be held accountable for their work.

But attitudes are changing. Younger people enter journalism now with little or no experience of unions. In fact, the media union, the Media, Entertainment & Arts Alliance (MEAA), now run workshops for trainee journalists or those emerging from journalism school to explain to them what a union does and what a strike or a picket line might mean to them. It seems remarkable to us that such briefings are necessary. We absorbed a union culture from our colleagues when we began our working lives. But in the past twenty years unions have lost members, power and visibility. They have been undermined by changes in the structure of the economy as well as legislation pushed by conservative politicians and commentators.

The stated political goal has been to make companies and the nation more competitive in the face of globalisation and emerging economies with cheaper wage structures. The argument was that if Australia were to maintain a strong economy, it had to get rid of unions or pull them into line. Powerful unions could force unsustainable wage deals and conditions.

But weakening unions also changed the power structure around work. For a start, many of the psychological barriers which held workers back from joining the corporate team were removed. Managers could present work as an activity that would fulfil employees rather than threaten them, release potential rather than block it. With union presence diminished in many workforces, there was now space for a competing philosophy about the nature of work. The reduction of union strength has given the corporate sector power not just to control demands for better wages and conditions but also to co-opt workers to its values and aims. There is room for a new cultural message to settle in the minds of workers, one that places employers in a far more positive light. It's also one that many workers seem happy to embrace. Work, as we have seen in earlier chapters, is a place where we can achieve, succeed, win personal satisfaction and meaning. It's not so easy for unions to demonise the boss in such a climate.

On the other hand, it's been easy to demonise unions as free-market opponents. On one side, the story goes, are old-fashioned unions; on the other the modern, rational market, the 'new economy' of the post-communist, 1990s world. American historian Thomas Frank argues in his book *One Market Under God* that the commentators and market boosters of this period created a world where 'workers who join unions are robots while workers who trade stocks on line are getting in touch with their humanity. We are willing, interactive participants in the funky, individualistic, ever-changing web of market democracy, *they* simply hear and obey.'[4]

The reduction of union power in Australia in the past few years has been surprising, given its big role in Australia's wage-fixing system from the early days of Federation. Unions sat alongside employers at the centralised industrial commissions which set wages at State and Federal level for almost ninety years. For generations the national wage case was as central to Australians' lives as any government policy or initiative. Workers awaited the outcome of the case with as much interest as they waited for Budget night to find out what taxes would fall or rise. The wage-fixing system was based on need – what a family with one wage earner needed for a basic existence. Philosophically, it was a world away from the market which, supposedly, rewards on merit, not need.

The centralised system was a radical method of equalising pay and distributing wealth. Unions, employers and governments cooperated in this system, driven by the belief that workers had a right to a basic level of pay as the starting point for their wages. In this context, employers were expected to be partners in the distribution of profits. Workers' demands were channelled through the unions, right to the centralised commission, and they often saw themselves as part of a community that went beyond their own workplaces and unions to a whole class of people, defined by their union background.

When one of us visited the big steel centre of Newcastle, north of Sydney, in 1999, the BHP operation there was closing and the city was gradually coming to terms with the shift away from a single, powerful unionised culture. But the old days seemed close to the surface as we talked to a young academic, Therese Davis, raised in Newcastle. She explained that as a child she had never shopped in the local branch of the David Jones department store chain. In fact, she confessed, she had never been in a DJs store until she left Newcastle and went to university in Sydney. 'There were certain stores I would not go into,' she said. 'We never went to David Jones. That store was not for the workers.'[5] Shopping at the co-op was about solidarity and identification with one's own class.

Newcastle was not the only place where such solidarity spilled into every corner of workers' lives. The stevedores who gave Chris Corrigan a rough time as he challenged their work practices on the docks had a union culture that included playing sport together, living cheek by jowl in places like Fremantle or the Rocks area of Sydney, sharing picnics, friendships and family connections. Work defined a sense of self.

Today, the old class structures are fading with the marginalisation of unions in many sectors and the demographic changes which make it hard to know who's a blue-collar worker any more. You may earn an average wage and work in the new 'assembly lines' of the call centre, but you are unlikely to define yourself as working class, and even less likely as a blue-collar worker. Instead, your status may be based more on what you choose to buy and the taste you demonstrate. The rise and rise of the middle class around the world is a big expansion of a consumer class, pushed by corporations and an economy that needs a mass market. Researchers have defined a new class, the 'aspirationals', who are motivated to purchase as a way of defining themselves. The brands they buy and the styles they seek are part of their upward social mobility.

In our own profession, union culture continues, even though it has been eroded by over-award payments and bonus schemes with the potential to divide newsrooms. Thirty years ago it was impossible to begin a career in journalism without joining the union – signing up to the Australian Journalists Association (later the MEAA) was automatic. No proprietor would even think of employing a journalist who was not a union member, so tight was the group. A handful of the most senior people on newspapers were 'exempt' from union membership. Each side agreed to this deal and 'exempt' staff were legally allowed to work during a journalists' strike, putting out thin versions of the paper stacked with 'black copy' or wire stories. It was unthinkable for any AJA member to break the strike or cross a picket line. Even reading the 'black' edition of the paper was frowned upon. This was the 1970s, before the introduction of new, computerised technology which would make publishing a doddle and remove an entire craft group from newspapers – the highly skilled linotype operators and printers. The printers' unions would eventually be destroyed by Rupert Murdoch's assault on them at his new plant at Wapping in East London in the 1980s, but their control of the industry, even in its more benign manifestation in Australia, was immense. These guys really could stop the presses. Printers were a group to be respected and feared, even by journalists who quickly learnt not to push the men in dust jackets with whom they worked late at night. We were all unionised, but the approach to work could not have been more different. They were upper crust, blue-collar workers, proud of their traditions but working strictly to rule. If it was time for their tea-break, they would take it, no matter that they were halfway through a task. We were low-level professionals, deadline junkies who regularly worked unpaid overtime and were often frustrated by the clock watchers. Sometimes we would try pleading with a printer to spend a couple of minutes to complete the make-up of a page for the presses before taking a scheduled break. Sometimes they would accede; sometimes they would ask the foreman to put someone else on to the page so they could still take their scheduled break. Mostly, we learnt that this was indeed a different country, where the printers heard a different drumbeat.

In the 1990s this would all change as journalists took over tasks previously carried out by those in the print union. The make-up of pages is now performed by journalists on the computers at their desks. Printers are no longer located downstairs or in an adjoining room but across the city in printing factories, their jobs restricted to running the heavily automated presses.

When we began in journalism, the AJA was keenly interested in a raft of work practices now seen to be solely the responsibility of the company. The AJA enforced ratios of staff on different grades, or pay levels. These requirements for proprietors to promote certain numbers of staff each year were written into industrial awards and were a way for the union to protect its members and ensure a distribution of people across pay scales. And the union was very interested in the proper training of journalists through the cadetship system, something which companies also took seriously. But no-one got far unless they joined the AJA.

In banks, unions historically covered everyone from clerks to branch managers. In the vast Australian outback, unions dominated big mining projects, and on the docks, nothing moved unless the union decided it should. Worker power was sometimes abused and some union officials were corrupt, but overwhelmingly, it was used well, to make sure people were paid, to make workplaces safe, to prevent arbitrary sackings and overt discrimination, and to ensure there was adequate training and that people moved through the pay scales at a reasonable rate. Australians absorbed a particular view of work which balanced labour and capital. There was a belief in collective action, and scepticism about the ability of the individual to survive in the system.

The extensive downsizings of the 1980s and early 1990s did little to encourage workers to believe they could go it alone. The union could not save their jobs, although many people found their only hope of a good redundancy package was in sectors where unions were still strong enough to negotiate. Unions forced concessions out of companies and governments in this period. It was the white-collar, middle managers who had never belonged to a union who suffered. They were often left with minimal payouts and no bargaining power with their employers, who suddenly dropped any sense of obligation to the Organisation Men.

But unions were not well placed to survive this period. Australia, like other Western democracies, was in the middle of economic and social change and a swing to the Right which would knock out many old allegiances. Culturally, the West was going through what social scientists term a 'de-alignment', a breaking away from the values of many traditional institutions. Union strength is patchy, strong in some areas like construction, coal mining, education and health and under stress in other areas like banking. But in the service sector and the information economy, in areas like sales and marketing, unions have been left far behind, with little ability to recruit members and shape workplace culture. At the same time, the Right has had great success in legislating to minimise union power and there is little or no constituency against such a trend.

The Hawke and Keating Labor governments that ran Australia from 1983 to 1996 kept unions in the loop through the historic Accord process which struck a balance between wage rises and a social contract, delivered by the government. The union movement itself, led by the innovative ACTU boss Bill Kelty, had attempted to move with the times by streamlining the members into fewer, bigger unions. The ACTU led the thinking around training and multi-skilling that was at the cutting edge of international ideas. It even moved towards a system of enterprise bargaining in which wages and conditions could be negotiated by unions directly with individual employers. This was a radical departure from the centralised wage-fixing system that had ruled in Australia for almost a century, under which industrial tribunals set wages and conditions. The move to relate wages more directly to profits of an enterprise is philosophically sound, for both sides, but the reality across the Australian workforce is apparent in variable outcomes. If your union is strong enough and your enterprise rich enough, you have done well enough in terms of wages. If not, you may have found yourself struggling to keep pace.

There are other factors affecting union power. From 1996, the Howard coalition governments sidelined the Australian Industrial Relations Commission (AIRC), cutting its power to intervene in or moderate enterprise-level outcomes. As well, the Federal Government's push for individual contracts has meant an increasing number of senior workers with a direct stake in management – creating divided loyalties that have reduced the power of unions.

But it is the development of the Human Resources staff in big corporations which is changing the culture of the workplace. A generation that has no idea about unions understands the role of Human Resources and how it relates to the organisation. It recognises, for example, that despite the best efforts of HR staff to play the honest broker role between workers and the company, HR answers to the boss. At the same time, HR is the source of training and cultural programs which promise management skills many workers hope will give them the edge in a competitive arena. For companies, often dismissive of HR in the past, such departments are now the engine room for embedding corporate values and goals into workers' hearts and minds.

The profession dates back to the early part of last century. The Ford factories of that era boasted sociological departments which were later transformed into personnel departments. These focused on the technicalities of hiring, firing, pay and leave, despite the yearning of their increasingly educated staffers to exercise more clout and corporate credibility.

Fifty years later, and personnel was still stuck on process rather than looking closely at the organisation of work or the workers. The 'father' of management theory, Peter Drucker, was the first to write about 'human resources' in his 1954 book *The Practice of Management*, in which he argued for a far broader role for it, one which looked across the spectrum of the way we work. The new title caught on but in many ways the shift in terminology during the 1960s and 1970s was not much more than a superficial name change, a reaction to Drucker's scathing assessment of the role of personnel management. 'Their preoccupation is with a "gimmick" that will impress their management associates,' he wrote.[6]

In the 1980s, as HR practitioners poured out of universities into big corporations, they faced a fresh barrier in their efforts to truly represent workers and, in a sense, replace the union. The next two decades would be dominated by the effort to move from a functional personnel role to a strategic one. But the downsizing and job re-organisation that cut through the Australian workforce at the time left the HR department dangling between the executive managers on one side and disaffected employees on the other. They were clearly exposed as unable to protect employees and in fact were often at the pointy end of the 'pink slips' atmosphere that dominated so many companies.

A decade on and HR is only just carving out a role for itself. The job, despite its name changes (these days the HR manager has often transformed into a people or knowledge manager), is often still focused on processes like recruitment, performance monitoring and pay, rather than influencing business strategy. It's true that many of the time-consuming and technical tasks like payroll and leave processing have been outsourced to specialist firms, yet the HR department often remains absorbed with process. The effort by HR to free itself up for a more strategic role in companies has not always been successful. Part of the problem is structural. When HR directors don't report into the senior executive group, their ability to influence is limited. Their promises to staff are often compromised and the role is left looking ineffectual, a mouthpiece for management.

Every HR manager wants a bigger role. When we interviewed a number of them for a special *AFR BOSS* at the end of 2002, we were struck by how keen they all were to position themselves at the board table. Each of them could see what was needed to make their jobs more relevant. The difficulty was getting there.

Sometimes they succeed in 'getting there' too well. Thomas Kochan, a leading HR academic who works at the Sloan School of Management at the Massachusetts Institute of Technology in Boston, suggests HR has let workers down by being so close to the executive suite that it has failed to challenge management ideas and decisions.

As executive salaries sky-rocketed in the past few years, Kochan noticed that there was no one at the table arguing on behalf of workers that the gap was just too large. In the US, the average pay of a CEO compared with the average worker's pay had exploded from a ratio of 40:1 in the 1960s and 1970s to more than 400:1 by 2003. Where were the HR directors when that imbalance was being created? Even more challenging for the profession was the fact that people issues were often not high on the agenda. Kochan cites a late 1990s survey of HR professionals which asked them to rank goals and priorities. The first six turned out to be around the needs of the organisation and the HR unit. 'The first workforce concern to make it on this list [promoting diversity] comes in seventh!' Kochan told a seminar at the University of Sydney in November 2003.[7]

The dream for the HR profession in the past few years was to 'partner' with line managers and senior executives in developing HR policies that supported the firm's competitive strategies, Kochan argues. In the process they became 'perfect agents' of top management – the alter egos of the boss, not the workers. That's a damning critique although one which many HR operators reject as they seek to work constructively with workers, and unions.

To some involved in organisational change, unions are a conduit to new cultures and practices, if they are included constructively in the exercise. Often the union is the only rallying point for workers and provides the emotional connection and the practical structures to introduce employees to new ideas.

Viv Read began working on the employer's side of IR in the 1970s. She argues that unions were once able to be the catalyst for change, with some of the big moves mediated through union-based structures. Getting the union onside was the big political challenge and a big step forward in changing cultures.[8] Consultant Bill Ford, who worked on a change program at the industrially complex Sydney Opera House in the late 1990s, argues that the involvement of unions in the process was crucial. Without them in an exercise like this, it would have been very much more difficult for management to engage the workers, he says.[9] The world-renowned building and tourist attraction had suffered for years from an 'us and them' culture and a history of strong unions. After all, workers had the Opera House management over a barrel, and many deals were made just before the curtain was due to go up on a performance. It took a few years and a determined Opera House boss in the shape of Michael Lynch (now at Southbank in London) to get a new deal through in late 2000 – in effect a single union and single enterprise agreement covering wages and conditions. The consultants worked closely with the various unions, setting up groups to work through key issues and move ahead.

We've been interested too in a program at Australia's largest airline, Qantas, where consultants have worked with the union in the maintenance section in an effort to change the culture. Here the emphasis has been on changing attitudes and improving communications between supervisors and other workers. An elaborate program was launched to break down entrenched attitudes and suspicion of management, who were also expected to change and become more collaborative. Outside consultants were hired to help run groups and exercises that would once have been ridiculed by unions as a management smoke screen. They were launched at a time when Qantas was trying to change working conditions, which it argued were financially unsustainable. It will take some time to see how the program pans out but it's an example of trying to achieve change by getting the union onside.

In her 2001 book *White Collar Sweatshop*, Jill Andresky Fraser suggests the new technology of the internet will link American workers in new ways. 'Websites clearly can be effective rallying devices, especially when organised around hot topics such as benefit cutbacks,' she says. 'When disgruntled employees at Bell Atlantic set up a chat room to discuss the company's cash-balance pension plan, they generated such an outpouring of complaints that they ultimately forced the company to negotiate a compromise with long-tenured employees.'[10] There are other examples in Australia too where unions have used the internet in recent years to build support on new sectors.

Even so, it's hard to escape the fact that the way unions are seen in Australian culture has shifted dramatically in the past thirty years. The union framework which supported workers – sometimes excessively, sometimes inadequately – has been dismantled bit by bit, leaving workers without the props that helped the weakest through the toughest times. Power has shifted and workers are increasingly on their own. For some, that's been liberating, as they use their own talent to achieve high wages and promotions. The end of demarcation lines, the opening up of jobs beyond corrupt closed shops: all these changes are welcome. In part, too, the growth of information workers and the knowledge economy means there is less need for unions to ensure physical safety, decent compensation and clean conditions. For many of the well-paid, work-engrossed professionals in our cities, unions are far from the main game: these workers are engaged in a power relationship with their organisations and they do not look to collective action as the mediating force.

Thirty years ago, one of the unwritten rules of the office, (even a professional office where we did not work to rule or knock off as soon as the clock struck 6 p.m.), was that one should not show up one's colleagues by working too hard. Working overtime without asking for time off and putting in too much effort were frowned upon, not because it might affect your health or happiness, but because of the damage it would do to others who would be expected by the boss to follow suit. It was one in, all in, and you had to do right by your colleagues in every sense of the word. To raise the bar was unsporting and you were advised to keep reasonably close to the pack. Those sentiments reflect a certain kind of Australian 'mateship', but they were also part of a union culture that looked for a homogeneous approach to flatten out the peaks and lows in the workforce. Workers were urged to fall into line and see the group as more important than making a splash with the boss. Today, that notion has evaporated as workers compete against each other for the boss's eye. To succeed, you must differentiate yourself, not disappear into the group. Our attitudes to work are no longer filtered through the lens of union values and goals. Rather, workers are encouraged to see themselves as having an individual relationship with their employer.

---

1. The Best Employers list is compiled annually by Hewitt Associates and the Australian Graduate School of Management. *AFR BOSS* is a media partner and the full list is published in the magazine each year.
2. The Australian Bureau of Statistics figures, published in *The Australian Financial Review.* 1 April 2003, p. 3.
3. Interview with Meaghan Morris.
4. Frank, Thomas. *One Market Under God: Extreme Capitalism, Market Populism and the End of Economic Democracy.* Vintage, 2000, p. xiv.
5. Trinca, Helen. 'No more bullied bloom', *The Sydney Morning Herald*, 29 September 1999, p. 12.
6. Drucker, Peter. *The Practice of Management.* Butterworth-Heinemann, 1999, p. 269. Originally published in 1954 by Harper.
7. Kochan, Thomas. 'Restoring trust in the Human Resource management profession', paper presented at Sydney University, November 2003.
8. Interview with Viv Read.
9. Interview with Bill Ford.
10. Andresky Fraser, Jill. *White Collar Sweatshop: The Deterioration of Work and its Rewards in Corporate America.* W.W. Norton & Company, 2001, p. 223.

5

Super Company:
is there another way?

Y<small>OU CAN'T HAVE A SEX LIFE AND</small> a full-time job, moans a thirty-something friend. He works very long hours to keep up in a highly competitive field, parents a lively two-year-old and has a deal with his partner to do some home duties. It's not unusual for him to be on the phone or working on his laptop at midnight.

At the big end of town, the CEO of a major institution, clearly at the peak of his career with enormous power and influence, tells us he is usually catatonic by the end of his working week – on Saturday afternoon.

This immersion in work can be hard to recognise when you are in the thick of it. Intense work brings its own pleasures, even if you do lose your libido. But to observers it can be a frightening spectacle. It can block intimacy – there is little time left over and no space for building relationships that are not about a commercial outcome. If you are intense about your work, how likely are you to need a private, personal relationship? How interested are you in the other side of life?

Not very, if our research is anything to go by. In her book *Baby Hunger*, about the absence of children among the female executive class, American researcher Sylvia Ann Hewlett describes the predicament of women who are too busy to even start a relationship, let alone a baby. Intimacy takes time and focus on the part of the participants, elements that companies prefer to see directed at their own projects. One of the women Hewlett talks to is simply grateful that she started dating her partner when they were at college and there was still time to get to know each other and build some sort of meaning and pattern into their relationship. They'd been living off that legacy for several years as they had become consumed by their careers. She wondered aloud whether they would even get to first base if they met for the first time now, in their grown-up, high-achieving phase.[1]

Anyone in the workforce will identify with some elements of these stories. Even family relationships, which are to all intents and purposes locked in, can come under serious assault as the players run out of emotional credit. Over and over senior executives have told us how appalled their children are by the lifestyle their 'successful' parents have chosen. 'I'm proud of you Dad,' said one teenager to his executive father, 'but I don't want to be like you.'

Maybe not, but the big organisation can deliver a level of success which that kid can scarcely imagine. For years we have seen the negatives of the big organisation and its strict timetables. From missing out on speech days at school to missing out on a sex life, work in the twenty-first century can flatten desire and drain energy. Even those getting a major buzz from their job can find there's not much left over for the rest of life by the time it comes to clocking off. Yet the rewards from working inside organisations are clearly deemed by many people to be worth the sacrifice.

In our own careers, organisations have given us the freedom to experiment with new ventures and develop our potential. Big organisations can provide a buffer zone and the financial security to experiment, and even sometimes to fail. For a start, the scale of big companies provides a structure where there is access to resources, information and support that is absent in smaller companies or for the self-employed. It's true that organisations have become leaner in recent years and that the pressure to succeed in short time-frames has intensified. But the safety net of the organisation is still real and something we understand and appreciate today far more than in the early stages of our working lives. In the 1960s and 1970s, only the nerds overtly embraced the system. For everyone else, the ideal was to break away, drop out, exit the rigid hierarchies and forge a more independent path outside 'Big Brother'. One day, some day, we'd all do a runner. It was inconceivable that the organisation would help you find yourself and become a better, bigger, more authentic you. You had to look for that in your outside life.

In reality most of our generation stuck it out, gradually being seduced by the notion that work was an important part of life, an end in itself. Sometimes that concession was based on the practicalities of financially supporting families and self. Sometimes it was about discovering a working life with challenges and rewards that have been 'better than sex' or at least an alternative to the chaos of domestic or private life. Sometimes it's been about the fear of working outside, as individuals, or not working at all.

Looking back, we can see how working inside the system has limited some aspects of our personalities and work experiences: there's always compromise when you operate within someone else's template. If we'd freelanced, or worked for less mainstream media organisations, we would, arguably, have challenged the system more. We might have developed different skills – for example, we might have become more entrepreneurial. But as journalists, it's difficult to find a way to publish ideas to a large, influential audience if you work outside the system. For us, being inside big organisations has given us a place to develop our craft and build a body of work.

But at times, employees find themselves on the defensive when it comes to working inside the system. Much of popular culture suggests the organisation is an unhappy spot to be. Think of Homer Simpson's battles at the plant. In recent years we have ploughed through books and interviewed a stack of people about the way organisations are failing their workers and need to change. The experts have told us over and over that a new generation wants a different sort of work environment, one that looks more like a warehouse with bean bags and operates more fluidly, if not anarchically. There's been a trend for women, in particular, to set up their own small businesses in a range of areas, part of a bid to circumvent companies that fail to promote them or make it hard for mothers to work there. To some commentators, it suggests a new world of workers finding their way into smaller operations or working from home as contractors, rather than in rigid, big organisations.

We remain unconvinced. Everything we see in our work and our daily lives seems to run counter to that notion. From where we sit, the organisation creaks and struggles but ultimately prevails. Individual companies, like Enron and HIH, have collapsed high and low in the past couple of years but don't confuse that with a collapse of the organisation as a model. In fact, the organisation as a way of marshalling talent and skill has never been more dominant in our society.

It's true that today's organisations are hollowed out: middle managers have all but disappeared, support staff like typists or secretaries and clerks are thin on the ground. Work can indeed look different now, but the organisation continues to exercise power and control behaviour, however ambiguous or glossed over. Big organisations have a momentum all their own. Just think of all the culture change programs that have struggled against the tendency for companies to stay as they are. Australia's banks have spent millions on organisational change with mixed results. It's not easy shifting sprawling organisations. In February 2004, Commonwealth Bank CEO David Murray said the goal of the bank's $1.7 billion change program was to get rid of bureaucracy – something he'd been trying to do since he got the top job in 1992.[2]

At the same time, many of us can't simply blame the company for the intensity of our working lives: it's often not overt power from the top that does the enforcing. There's as much likelihood that the fever to work hard is coming from inside, so successfully has the ethic been internalised.

We spoke in detail to Leigh Clapham, the general manager of MasterCard International, Australasia, about work, career and the big changes. He spent much of his career in the advertising world, eventually running a major agency and then switching to his present role in a multinational. After almost thirty years in the workforce he has seen enormous changes in what's expected and delivered at the office. These days, he finds that people in companies don't push their authority as much as they used to. 'People are more likely to say "I work with someone", rather than "I am their boss",' Clapham says. 'There's a more egalitarian approach to people working together. I think it's a very good thing as long as the ultimate authority is known and respected. You still need those levels of authority to get things done.'[3]

Today's employees certainly don't need as many prompts or commands, and indeed there are far fewer layers of management to hand out the orders. But recognition of the authority structure remains a given for workers. And most modern employees are still partly chained to the organisation. There may indeed be a weightless economy where people wring value from moving information and ideas about, but the organisation is still remarkably powerful.

The fact that so many of us are still at the office or behind the counter in an age of increased mobility and communication shows the endurance of the organisation. Most of us take it as given that the organisation is the best structure for work and it's so embedded in our psyche there's little space for alternatives. The organisation that pulls most of us into the workplace every day is rarely seen as a construct resulting from a range of social and historical forces. Most of us turn up to work rather than telecommuting or freelancing, for example, because it seems that is the best way to get the job done, as Leigh Clapham explains: 'A lot of roles require physical presence and there's a great deal of the conformist in us. My colleagues could think I am sitting at home doing nothing if I'm not here. I think we do define our jobs by our presence.

'But I think there is an overwhelming issue, which is why it still happens today the way it happened thirty years ago – why we commute and go to the office, we work together and go home. It's efficient, it works and you get the job done. I think there is a far greater risk if I said to people here, work at home whenever you like. I have a distinct concern that their level of contribution and efficiency would go down rather than stay at the level it is. They are not trained for it, the office isn't there and the temptation is always there. It's not that I distrust anyone, but out of the office where everything is happening there'll always be things you miss. Someone will look for you and you're not there, or walk into an office to show you something. So the work environment is the most efficient environment.'

There are other reasons why we often feel most comfortable in the office, whether we are the boss or more junior. There's a very clear link between the office and status and identity. To be a conspicuous player in the work environment, where you can see and be seen, pushes work to the centre of your life. In a corporate environment, you need to be at work to be a player, so it's not surprising that it can dominate our sense of self. Holding people to an office structure may well be more efficient but it also minimises the time and opportunity to develop individual interests or pursue intimate relationships. The organisational experience overtakes individual experience.

The organisation is a given but it is not static and has gone through various stages. Andrew Jones, an anthropologist at the University of Alabama, says we are now in the corporate stage of cultural evolution.[4] We have moved through other stages – bands, tribes, chiefdoms and states – to the fifth stage: the corporate. The people who inhabit our corporations and the decisions they make colour our lives and language. Writer Kate Jennings urges novelists to explore the business world, for 'to ignore moguls, exec-utives, bureaucrats, working stiffs – their sorrowing, enthusiasms, contradictions, frustrations, scheming – is to ignore a large chunk of our world.'[5] In his book *Death Sentence*, Australian writer Don Watson blames corporate culture for ruining public language. Words like 'accountable' are now used by footballers; women and men talk about getting 'closure' after a love affair; and from every boardroom and marketing department there comes unabashed and ungrammatical rubbish that degrades the country's vocabulary and attitudes.[6]

Jennings, too, has written about the horrors of corporate language and the way it is used to mask the truth in business or distance individuals from reality. In the workplace, talking the talk is a matter of survival. So pervasive has the language of 'bottom lines' (results) and 'take-outs' (key points made at a meeting or briefing) become that not to use such words marks you as either unsophisticated or subversive. Acceptance and promotion depend in large part on your willingness to adopt the corporate language. But the way such language has seeped into our private lives is even more extraordinary. It is yet another way in which the line between public and private is blurred, another way in which work dominates our world. In this sense, corporates have used language to help them colonise the rest of our lives. There is no escape from our jobs if we use the same words to talk about our love affairs as we use for a morning conference discussion.

From the start of the twentieth century when sociologists began to focus on a theory of organisation, the company was seen as a machine and the goal was to make it run smoothly. In his classic *Images of Organization*, published in 1986, Gareth Morgan argues that the 'design of organisations [was seen] as a technical problem'.[7] Humans had to fit in with the mechanical organisation. The focus was on big-scale, standardised production and a 'scientific approach' to management, as developed by Frederick Winslow Taylor. Companies broke down work into precise tasks able to be performed by illiterate or unskilled workers. Tasks were handed out to the workers by those who planned the operations. Responsibility went in the opposite direction – a key part of scientific management was to 'shift all responsibility for the organisation of work from the worker to the manager'.[8] Managers had to think, workers had to implement. Scientific management was as much about controlling workers as about making them productive.

Cogs in a wheel? Modern management theory and practice encourages bosses and supervisors away from such politically incorrect thoughts. Instead, those who are charged with leading others at work these days are invited to think of the organisation as a place where people can demonstrate their knowledge and creativity. Lynda Gratton, associate professor of organisational behaviour at the London Business School, wrote a book in 2000 called *Living Strategy: Putting People at the Heart of Corporate Purpose*.[9] The title describes much of the present thinking about people as core business assets, as individuals who must be understood and nurtured.

One of the most powerful management ideas of the past twenty years is the notion of the 'learning organisation', developed by Peter Senge. His argument, outlined in classic books like *The Fifth Discipline*, is that the organisation must drop the 'command-and-control' model and see itself as a living entity with the capacity to learn.[10] Other commentators talk of the need to see companies as 'living organisms' able to unleash the creativity of those who work in them. At one level it seems obvious. Organisations are groups of people who together invent rituals (like Christmas parties, cakes on employees' birthdays or weekly assemblies) and pass on values (like industriousness). But there's a strong countervailing view, which sees companies as well-oiled machines that should aspire to operate efficiently, rather than creatively. Organisations find it hard to accommodate the things that make us human – the vagueness, the ambivalence, the messiness – and they do not reward such behaviour. They do not easily give way to individuals. Small, entrepreneurial organisations or start-ups may be flexible, but big organisations run to set rhythms that can be difficult to recalibrate.

We have talked to CEOs and senior managers about the changes they are trying to make to their company ethos and culture and have learnt quickly that despite the talk there is a real problem in actually allowing the workplace to operate differently. Even when creativity is the goal, most executives admit privately that they do not tolerate mistakes, a natural concomitant of experimenting. Inherent in the organisation is the notion that it controls, or at least arranges, the behaviour of its members.

When we talked to specialists involved in a big culture change program at the National Australia Bank it was clear that ideas that looked fine on paper were often difficult in practice.[11] The bank's hierarchical structure resulted in a series of silos which struggled to communicate or work together.

The power of the organisation can be seen in the extent to which it eats up our energy. Having cut the middle out of the corporation in the 1980s and 1990s companies now expect that those remaining in jobs simply do more. Six years after writing his book, Gareth Morgan tells us: 'I don't know of any sector where people aren't working a hell of a lot harder than they were – and it seems to be getting worse. It's almost as if the [machine metaphor] is being reinvented in a new way, with the new technology.'[12]

Leigh Clapham finds he has little time between appointments. His diary is packed. 'My day starts at about 7.45 in the office – it's emails, first twenty minutes, and getting a list of things to do for the day. That's if I haven't written it the day before. Then I spend ten minutes with my secretary giving her the priorities for the day. Then it descends into a nightmare of meetings. Having a regional office in Singapore means I sometimes have very long phone discussions – up to two hours. My diary is normally extremely full – this week hasn't even really started and I've got a meeting every hour every day of the week.' It's close to 8 p.m. by the time he gets home; just time enough to sit down for dinner with his wife and teenage sons.

Clapham's example shows that there is now significant order and structure in our working lives. Often every moment is accounted for by the appointment diary and you must be able to juggle several tasks. Yet this gives you more control over your time at work than you can achieve in your personal life. And being busy is a no-brainer when it comes to status in the office. To be busy is to be part of the world of serious work. You are central to the project, needed and fulfilled in ways not always open to you in your personal life.

The pressure has grown enormously in recent years. Clapham has seen the shift over the decades he has spent in the workforce, especially in the 1990s. 'The capacity of senior individuals in authority to be involved and influence and do more has grown exponentially in the past seven or eight years. The number of things I get involved in in a day, either through email, or phone or face to face, is enormous.' Much of it is due to technology and the fact that we can all be contacted anytime, anywhere. A few years ago, says Clapham, you thought you should work quickly; now you figure you had better do it immediately: 'Everything is half an hour.' Once, he assumed staff would turn around a request or project in three days. Now he expects it the same day. Multiply that demand for speedy responses throughout the organisation and you get some sense of the intensity now experienced by more and more people.

In the 1970s and even the 1980s, reporters in a city newsroom, for example, might be required to cover one or two events or issues each day. Today, they work on several projects at once, with a range of short-, medium- and long-term deadlines.

The incredible 'tightness' of organisations caused by reduced staff and demands to produce more, the lack of slack, means that there is little support for workers. Slack, of course, doesn't refer to doing nothing, although there are millions of ways to get away with that in the short-term. Slack or downtime include thinking space and time for debate and discussion, a chat with a colleague from another division – the kinds of actions that used to be part of organisational membership. Gareth Morgan says that the 'great thing about the hierarchy was that there was always somewhere to pass the work, but that isn't allowed any longer, the capacity isn't there'.[13] The structure is so skeletal that workers are left to sink or swim, without the traditional buffer of their colleagues. They must get through their load alone.

It adds up to a flashpoint for an often emotional, at times desperate conversation in many parts of the world. Its impact on families, sex and intimacy, health, stress levels and time for community interaction is increasingly documented. But it's evident to us that notwithstanding the changes in the organisation – the increased flexibility, the flattening of layers of management and the demands it can make on workers – have increased, not decreased.

Many workers are now driven, subject to tighter controls and 'monitored to death'. Far from being creative, workers can find themselves with less space than ever because they are so visible. The nature of modern work is empowering with its emphasis on individual responsibility. It's something that hooks you in and makes you feel good about work and yourself. But at the same time, the responsibility means increased accountability with all the checks and balances and controls imposed by companies to quantify and validate your output. It's a confusing mix at times and for workers who don't measure up, there's very little room to move and nowhere to hide. We have seen this in some organisations where we have worked, which have traditionally been able to 'carry' employees who were either not quite up to it – ill, stressed or not coping. It was not just unions who kept people in jobs. Decent middle managers would often find ways to keep people on the books, recognising that not everyone was created equal in the great work race. Today's workplace gives even the most benevolent manager little scope when it comes to protecting workers. An 'up or out' attitude permeates many professional services firms, for example. There is no room for the merely average, or the passengers, as one HR manager described them. This is particularly so in the private sector where it is much easier to dump workers than it is in the public sector. In both sectors there are few places where people can be parked out of sight of the number crunchers.

Then there are those on the frontline – the troops staffing the phones, serving the shoppers, keeping the customers happy. It can feel like going into battle and military terminology seems appropriate to describe the tactics and drama of these jobs. Keeping customers happy has always been part of the transaction between producer and consumer. But it used to be the boss who had to worry about losing contracts. Now everyone is responsible. Customer relations have flooded down to the lowest level in the workplace, and companies have shifted the duty of care down the line. Junior workers are asked to think strategically about clients and to be engaged in the process. Many jobs have been made more interesting because workers have to engage more directly with clients. At times it also means more dealings with managers and potentially more access to information. No CEO can afford to ignore this thirst for contact. If employees don't get it from the top, they can find it out for themselves on the internet. The upshot is workers often feel they are a real part of the drive for success and profits. That direct involvement comes with a loss of the traditional protection from market forces. Employees are paid a lot less than the boss but they are expected to make a significant emotional connection and take responsibility for the company's viability. Yet the lure of more responsibility is part of the attraction of many jobs. Many employees can't wait to help carry the load, as a way of differentiating themselves from peers and being noticed.

For a company, capturing the emotional energy of an employee is seen as a huge plus. Of course this investment – a kind of psychological identification with the organisation – can go too far and leave an unhealthy legacy, particularly if jobs are being cut. If you're dedicated to IBM and think it's for the long term, losing your job is a personal as well as a professional blow. We've noticed a number of warnings appearing about the risks of too much emotional investment in work.

Organisations, however, have a big investment in encouraging you to deny your private life and look to work for the energy and excitement of play and intimacy. They don't easily cope with the personal lives of workers and are more comfortable when you embrace the company mission. The intensity of modern workplaces makes it easy to forget that there's potential for another way of being, a world of personal relationships, interests, the arts, sport, intimacy – and even sex.

While sex is out, 'culture' is in. If we had a dollar for every time we have heard the phrase 'cultural change program' in recent years, we'd be a rich duo by now. Cultural change is the mantra of modern organisations. By the early 2000s even CEOs were openly talking up cultural change programs, not just to make their HR department happy, but in a bid to woo the financial analysts whose views on a company can affect its share price. John Akehurst, the then CEO of Woodside, told us in May 2003 that culture – the ethos, attitudes and values of the company – made the difference when fund managers were tossing up between companies that were otherwise identical.[14] The idea is that if your company is seen to have an inclusive culture, for example, or one which rewards talented people, you will be marked positively compared with one which exhibits a ruthless approach to staff or is extremely hierarchical. We're sceptical of the capacity of an analyst who is often basing ideas on financial numbers to get a handle on the internal culture of a company, but the stampede is on. Culture, the CEOs and boards are told, will make a difference to your productivity and to how you are perceived outside.

But culture is complex and squishy and dependent on ad hoc factors, such as particular managers. When it's imposed, either by the HR department, outside consultants, or the executive team, it can fail to have the desired effect. It can also change rapidly. Today's blokey office can shift to a more inclusive zone with a collaborative boss, and back again the other way when a new woman or man walks in the door. The problem with many contemporary cultural change programs is that they are essentially instrumentalist in approach – the company wants a prescribed outcome. It wants workers to adopt certain values, ethics and behaviour. It may be excellent behaviour but this is not democratic and workers are not volunteering, no matter what spin is attached. Organisations will argue strongly that they do not want to be dogmatic about culture but they are being disingenuous – any effort to shift culture in the office is about an imposition of certain ideas from above.

Are we being too negative about the potential for organisations to share the power with their employees? Surely, companies voted as Best Employers or those who overtly seek to become 'employers of choice' are providing more opportunities and a better environment for staff? Isn't it the case that the organisation is mutating, reinventing itself for the twenty-first century as a response to a more highly educated, creative, autonomous labour force?

Yes and no. The first thing to make clear is that organisations are not of themselves malevolent. Much of what happens around the way corporations run is accidental. But the sheer scale of corporations means that they create and impose structures on those they employ. This is not necessarily a conscious process.

The second point is that there are some new forms of organisation emerging. Gareth Morgan says we are seeing a lot of entrepreneurship and the new companies are much smaller.[15] The decentralisation of activities is also having an impact on the way companies operate. The pressure on resources translates into different structures, the most obvious being the reduction in bureaucracy. Some of the most interesting organisations of recent years have been created by entrepreneurs who do things differently. One that is often quoted is Flight Centre, the successful airline travel retailer developed by one of Australia's brightest operators, Graham Turner, Australia's answer to Richard Branson. Flight Centre employs some 6,000 people around the country and overseas, employees who are widely seen as contented, committed and motivated. Turner is a rich man, but he is rewarded on the same remuneration basis as his employees.

In their article in *The Journal of Industrial Relations* in September 2002, academic researchers Ian Palmer and Richard Dunford looked at some of the reasons for the success of this company. Dunford says that Flight Centre has realised that selecting the right people, training them and keeping them happy, is better than simply being a 'terminus with people passing through'. He sees Flight Centre's care around recruitment, its stress on performance pay and other behaviour, as very positive. And one of the other things that Turner has got right is the balance between the individual and the group. People who don't fit into the culture are often labelled 'sharks' by their colleagues, Dunford tells us. The 'sharks' are highly competitive and work hard to be individually rewarded under the Flight Centre system. But they don't get the second half of the equation – that the company's success is dependent on co-operation and teamwork.[16] Flight Centre pays a retainer with incentives, according to its global HR manager Mark Aponas. But there's also a profit share system for team leaders that helps drive them to produce a result.[17]

This tension between the individual and the group is one of the most challenging issues for any organisation and for every manager. Fifty years ago, there was no question the group was dominant. William H. Whyte's *The Organization Man* is the classic work which describes and critiques what the author saw as excessive conformity within organisations. He writes about the famous book *The Caine Mutiny*, by Herman Wouk. The novel, also made into a film, tells of a sailor who goes against his bullying captain in order to save the lives of those on board. But Wouk's message is that the sailor was wrong to follow his conscience. He should have followed the group rules, because to challenge authority is to risk anarchy.

Today's manager has more obvious tensions to deal with, and no easy way to find a balance between team effort and individual talent and ambition. Looking after yourself and your needs pervades our society. Companies measure individual output through performance reviews while workers struggle for the point of difference from others so that they can stand out from the group long enough to get that next promotion.

In many ways, organisations come between workers and their work. So much popular culture around work, from Dilbert cartoons to the British television show *The Office*, ridicules the boss and the organisation, not the work itself. The comedy comes from the stupidity of bureaucracies or middle managers, not the honest deployment of your effort to make a living. Researcher Carl Rhodes has looked closely at worker identity in corporate culture and how it is stylised in popular culture, and says that invariably people are critical of organisations. It is a constant in his field of work, this discovery of complaints about the system.[18]

By and large, people are not anti-work but they are very often anti-organisation. They will search for meaning in what they do but sneer at the latest corporate culture program; look for ways to streamline their job but pay little attention to management edicts; invest their own time and money in career advice and decide when and for how long they will give their allegiance to an organisation. Rhodes, who worked in human resources at Citigroup before entering academia, says movies like *Blade Runner* pit the individual against the villainous organisation but even shows as subversive as *The Simpsons* do not attack work. Rather it is the plant that is the bogey and the plant owner who is Homer Simpson's nemesis.

For us as writers in this area, there is little doubt the organisation remains a robust entity with the power to influence our lives deeply. In that sense, many of the claims made for alternatives have failed to materialise. Most of us continue to work in companies that have found it hard to change their systems of operating, even when there is interest in doing so. Not all of this is bad. We've seen big companies delivering not just pay packets but great fulfilment and growth to employees. The firm can be a great place to work. Witness the fervour of Virgin Blue employees who love the flexibility and engagement with their airline.

It's also clear there are big social forces, in particular the presence of both parents in the workforce, that will continue to modify the way organisations run. Redesigning jobs to take them out of the nine-to-five template or, better still, out of the 24/7 approach, is something that corporations have resisted. But it seems unlikely they will be able to continue this absolutism indefinitely. There are other changes likely too, as the Baby Boomers age but refuse to give up their jobs. Organisations could well shift the way they operate to maintain these people in some way, and there will be political and social pressure to do so. Already the Federal Public Service has adopted guidelines for more flexible working arrangements, allowing, for example, older people to stay on but in less senior positions.[19] The organisation is an organic entity and will continue to evolve.

Then there's the pressure from the 'flash mobbers' and the 'knowledge workers' who could well create less structured offices. We have already seen dramatic changes from the participation of women in work. The dynamics of work were traditionally male-dominated in many sectors but the presence of women, not as clerical staff or assistants but as equals and superiors, has shifted the way people deal with each other.

There is certainly no shortage of ideas about what should happen to the organisation. A whole genre of management books and articles has been published in the past fifty years examining work, jobs, careers and alternatives to the traditional models. There is a thirst for analysis and reflection on work, illustrated in the calls we get about articles in *AFR BOSS*, the extraordinary popularity of *Fast Company* (which at one stage rivalled upmarket glossies, like the now defunct *Talk* magazine, in the United States) and the sales of books like *Free Agent Nation* by Daniel Pink and *What Should I Do With My Life?* by Po Bronson. Much of this material crosses between work and life, giving a very clear indication of the focus many workers now have on making sense of both, not just tolerating one and enjoying the other. There is a pressure on the organisation to better meet the expectations of employees. It's not so easy to dismiss the commentators who argue for change.

This body of literature is not all about dropping out of working life either. The idea of a 'sea change' or downshifting by reducing work is a useful option for only a limited number of people. Far more must stay in full-time work for financial or emotional reasons, so much of the current thinking is about injecting something new into an existing structure to make it change.

In his book *Loyalty Rules! How Today's Leaders Build Lasting Relationships*, Frederick F. Reichheld urges managers to 'create heroes and heroines' in their organisations to increase commitment from employees.[20] In *Funky Business*, Swedish academics Jonas Ridderstråle and Kjell Nordström argue the case for nurturing creativity and attracting talented staff to ensure your future competitiveness. They talk of building networks within organisations and between organisations as a way of staying up to date and keeping pace with a new generation which builds elaborate personal networks to help them cope with surging information and demands.[21] Thomas Davenport and John Beck focus on the 'attention economy' in their book of the same name, suggesting companies can be renewed by paying some attention to the way employees manage the flood of information that swirls around today's organisation.[22] Peter Senge's work on the 'learning organisation', the idea that you can reconfigure the way organisations operate by engaging workers in new ways, is another classic example of efforts in the past twenty years to shift structures within the traditional full-time system.[23]

Often individuals make these interventions themselves. When English journalist and author Richard Donkin got fed up with the politics and pain of the office, he left. On extended leave from his position at the *Financial Times*, he wrote a book called *Blood Sweat and Tears: The Evolution of Work.* It was only when he broke away from a structured workplace that he was able to thoroughly research his topic: his research and writing merged into his personal quest to find a satisfying and practical way of earning a living within the constraints of the market. When we spoke to Donkin in 2003, he had been away from full-time, office-based work for several years and was freelancing for the *Financial Times*. He's not alone in this decision to work from home. He was lucky, his paper supported him, but organisations rarely initiate such moves – the telecommuter is not the preferred employee for companies because marshalling workers into one spot is easier.[24]

Demand from employees and commentators for autonomy remains a pressure point for organisations. In fact, the knowledge economy may well provide options for greater freedom within organisations. If the key to productivity is increasingly knowledge, then the dynamics of an office change. Managers need to extract intellectual property from their workers who thus find themselves in the box seat. Even before he went freelance, Richard Donkin found working for the *Financial Times* with several editors meant developing transactional relationships with them. If he had an idea for a story, Donkin would think about getting the best coverage and space for it by negotiating with the managers – the editors – who were better to deal with and more sympathetic. Unpopular editors were avoided.

This sort of relationship between employee and manager can dissolve demarcation lines. As Donkin found, people will gravitate to better managers; the ones who treat them well and respect their ideas. But it's a model that hinges on the sharing of power and the ability of the worker to sell his or her skills to different 'customers'. Not many managers react well to ceding power, whether it will give them better results or not. And many occupations simply don't lend themselves to this approach, particularly if a formal hierarchy remains in place. But supervisors with better reputations will attract 'volunteers' rather than conscripts for projects. Workers, as a result, can become more commercial about their jobs even as they stay on the payroll. Get that equation right and workers have a clear sense of how they fit in and the value of what they do. It's a little like co-opting the motivation of a small business owner for the salaried employee.

Kjell Nordström touches on a more literal definition of the commercial worker. He believes the Marxist idea of workers owning the means of production is already happening in organisations.[25] Some corporations are being forced to give their top talent options or employee share schemes to keep their knowledge in-house. Nokia is already 25 per cent owned by employees. But share ownership alone will not shift the cultures of big organisations running to tight schedules and using systems which minimise individual choice. A company can be owned by the workers through share schemes, yet at the same time have no real sense of ownership.

We've seen other ways it can work – albeit in a limited way. In our office, where a small team works on the monthly magazine *AFR BOSS*, we have noted the sense of autonomy and community a sub-unit can have in a large organisation. It is possible for these hubs to provide the cultural advantages of smaller companies with the opportunities and resources of larger businesses. Some of the benefit is illusory, after all, decisions can be vetoed and approval must be sought for new directions. But the sub-unit can provide the haven that a commercial worker needs to operate effectively.

The push-pull between the individual and the company is far from resolved. As we suggested, the organisation is a powerful beast, not easily put down, and it is able to lay down the rules – even in an economy so dependent on the ideas and creativity of employees. One area where there is still little give is in the way the corporation measures value and payment. Richard Donkin finds it ridiculous, for example, that employees should have to work a forty-hour week if they can get the work done in twenty hours. He blames a 'managerial greed that says, "if you can do it in twenty hours you can do twice as much in forty hours"'.[26] Yet the entrepreneur doesn't work that way and Donkin argues that individuals too must become more entrepreneurial and individualistic in their thinking. This could prove to be unrealistic. Autonomy is good news for individuals but tricky for companies who need a degree of conformity to operate efficiently. And as Leigh Clapham says, the system works, for all its faults.

---

1. Hewlett, Sylvia Ann. *Baby Hunger: The New Battle for Motherhood.* Atlantic Books, 2002.
2. Boyd, Tony. 'Murray's crusade: banish bureaucracy', *The Australian Financial Review*, 14–15 February 2004, p. 10.
3. Interview with Leigh Clapham. All further quotations from Clapham come from this interview.
4. Jones, Andrew. 'Managing the gap', *Organizational Dynamics*, Vol. 32, Number 1, 2003, pp. 17–31.
5. Jennings, Kate. Address to the Sydney Institute, 29 April 2003.
6. Watson, Don. *Death Sentence: The Decay of Public Language*, Knopf, 2003.
7. Morgan, Gareth. *Images of Organization.* Sage Publications, 1986, p. 35.
8. Ibid. p. 28.
9. Gratton, Lynda. *Living Strategy: Putting People at the Heart of Corporate Purpose.* Financial Times Prentice Hall, 2000.
10. Senge, Peter. *The Fifth Discipline: The Art and Practice of the Learning Organisation.* Currency, 1990.
    Senge, a former engineer, reinterpreted management practice using the application of system thinking to develop the idea of a learning culture for a knowledge-based economy. Senge, who works at the Sloan School of Management at the Massachusetts Institute of Technology, argues that organisations should be built around five core elements – systems

thinking, shared visions, team learning, mental models against which to test assumptions, and personal mastery.

11. The culture programs run by the National Australia Bank were outlined in interviews with bank staff in 2003 and 2004.
12. Interview with Gareth Morgan.
13. Ibid.
14. Trinca, Helen. 'The Woodside experiment: lose the fear', *AFR BOSS*, Vol. 4, Number 8, p. 28.
15. Interview with Gareth Morgan.
16. Dunford, Richard and Palmer, Ian. 'Managing for high performance? People management practices in Flight Centre', *The Journal of Industrial Relations*, September 2002, pp. 376–396.
17. Interview with Mark Aponas.
18. Interview with Carl Rhodes.
19. Hepworth, Annabel. 'PM's plan to make you work longer', *The Australian Financial Review*, 2 December 2003, p. 1.
20. Reichheld, Frederick F. *Loyalty Rules! How Today's Leaders Build Lasting Relationships*. Harvard Business School Press, 2001, p. 182.
21. Nördstrom, Kjell and Ridderstråle, Jonas. *Funky Business: Talent Makes Capital Dance*. Financial Times Prentice Hall, 1999.
22. Davenport, Thomas H. and Beck, John C. *The Attention Economy: Understanding the New Currency of Business*. Harvard Business School Press, 2001.
23. Senge, op cit.
24. Interview with Richard Donkin.
25. Fox, Catherine. 'The new manifesto', *AFR BOSS*, Vol. 4, Number 7, p. 58.
26. Interview with Richard Donkin.

6

Working with attitude: getting into the mode

THE NEWSROOM OF A NATIONAL daily newspaper doesn't seem a likely place to successfully forge a new template for flexible work. Deadlines, news conferences, daily turnaround, last minute upheaval – how could this apparent chaos cope with anything less than full-time effort and full-time hours? As journalists we work in an environment where part-time work has been an option for employees for a number of years. In fact, ten years ago, when one of us put the system to the test, there was an eventual agreement to a four-day week, then three days. It was pretty much accepted that the part-time role had to be other than a front-line reporting job, which are generally seen to require full-time hours, if not more.

Most part-timers in those days worked on weekly sections of *The Australian Financial Review* (*AFR*) or wrote features, so their deadlines for submitting their work were a little longer. Daily news coverage involves unpredictable hours. When a big news story happens it's harder for a part-time worker to stay back late to get the first stories written if they have other deadlines to meet in their 'outside of work' life. But there are plenty of other roles on a daily newspaper that don't require this kind of flexibility.

Nearly all the part-time workers were, and still are, women, although at least one man opted to drop his hours in order to spend less time commuting. Over a few years some interesting and subtle changes have occurred. The assumptions about what was possible in part-time hours and the level of commitment involved changed. It was a slow process, but eventually some journalists returning from maternity leave went back to news reporting in key areas of the newspaper. The understanding was that they would, for example, do three days of reporting on their round, with colleagues assisting on the days they were not at their desk. It was not always a smooth process but gradually it was seen to work. The *AFR* retained some talented journalists, who in turn kept jobs they enjoyed and the years of experience and knowledge they had gained was used as leverage.

It's not perfect and dismissive attitudes to part-timers still surface. Part-time work is still a reward that you earn by performing well for many years as a full-time employee. It's difficult to change established patterns and there's little give in the typical business structure where long hours signal you are serious about your career. Part-time workers battle to prove they are 'on board'. The progress made by the *AFR* has certainly not blinded us to the stark reality of most workplaces. Having first-hand experience of switching to part-time work has made a number of issues clear to us. Many assumptions made about the commitment to the company are based on the hours spent at the desk. If the output of a job is clear and tangible, such as articles in a newspaper, the notion that you are only as good as the hours invested in the job can be challenged. But in many cases the equation is not so straightforward and measuring the results can be far from clear. An unspoken but pervasive value of the twenty-first-century organisation is that you can't possibly be serious about your job unless you're working long hours. As the pressure to work harder and faster increases there's been a corresponding paranoia about the level of commitment to the job. One of the most obvious manifestations is sensitivity about the hours spent at work. Employees at many organisations know the score only too well – if you're not at your desk until the boss leaves you're playing with fire, and going part-time is suicide.

No wonder the topic of part-time work touches a raw nerve. It's a logical answer if a drop in income can be sustained, but it gets a bad rap whenever the debate about long work hours and dedication to the job comes up. Our analysis and first-hand experience – plus comments from dozens of colleagues, peers and contacts who assured us that part-time work could *never* succeed in their office – has made it clear. Part-time work is usually a bad career move no matter what the quantity and quality of the work produced.

The politics of how part-time work became part of an unpopular ghetto is another grim reminder of the strength and dominance of organisational structures, and indeed the market. Just a few years ago, both these alternatives were viewed positively as the answer to concerns about stress, parenting, balance and even unemployment. Our own experience certainly backs this up. Moving from full-time work certainly made a major difference and allowed one of us to continue in the workforce instead of opting out altogether. It was lucky the option was there, many friends commented. Gratitude seemed to be expected by the workplace and the assumption was that the effort invested in the job would be very high to justify the rewarding of part-time status. These days part-time is shorthand for casual, low-status work that many women are forced to take once they become parents. Or if it's part of the language of work/life balance, it's informally regarded as a low-status option for slackers.

As the HR manager in a large professional services firm told us, the managers in the organisation immediately react with suspicion to any suggestion of flexibility, much less part-time work. Despite paying lip service to company policies on work/life balance, informally they worry it may set an unhealthy precedent, it's disrupting for the flow of work, or others will be resentful. Part-time work is disparaged by many employees and managers alike. Some managers regard it as troublesome to administer, disruptive and a sneaky way of getting out of doing your job properly. It makes them uneasy. But colleagues can find it disturbing too, often feeling they are picking up the pieces left behind when the part-timer clocks off. In recent years, as downsizing has continued to slowly erode the workforce, these complaints have multiplied. The manager of a twenty-strong team in a large organisation we interviewed about job-sharing said since the concept was introduced in his workplace he had fielded numerous complaints from his workers who felt they were carrying an extra burden. The real problem was that the two employees sharing a job were each expected to cover many of the tasks of their former full-time roles. Instead of sharing one job they were effectively being asked or expected to fill full-time positions in their part-time hours.

Many employees can see right through this, all their worst fears about rhetoric rather than reality borne out by the practice. And they are right to worry about part-time work when the organisation expects so much for less. But there are other factors at play. Many workers are on the record with their desire for more free time and their willingness to sacrifice pay. But even if the opportunity to work part-time presents itself many find they simply can't give up full-time status. The power that work bestows often overrides the attraction of a more manageable personal life with time for relationships and intimacy.

A friend tells us that her life is pretty unbearable with the struggle to keep her family on track and the demands of her senior role at a leading financial services firm. And she admits taking the part-time option would represent a sign of defeat for her. 'I've worked so hard to get here,' she says. 'I know that if I wanted to work part-time it would be seen as stepping off the career path and taking a back seat. Even if there was a job I could do.' She has heard the remarks of colleagues about those who have taken this route and watched them disappear from meetings and strategy discussions. It doesn't take much, she points out, to get sidelined.

Her perception is that a change to her full-time status would also be a sign to her peers and the industry that she was no longer interested in moving ahead. Watching others in her workplace switch to part-time work has helped cement this belief. She admits that her sense of self and achievement and her identity are at risk of being unbearably eroded by such a step. She believes it would be better in some ways to resign and leave the workforce completely than to switch to part-time work. Her feelings are reinforced by indirect feedback from management. Part-time work equals workplace invisibility, and is mainly chosen by women, which has helped to lower its status even further. When a lawyer at a leading firm announced she was trading a full-time role for three days a week, she was shocked by the behaviour of colleagues. Some actually walked past her in the corridor without acknowledging she was there. It's interesting that the stigma of part-time work sticks even when it's clear that the employee's output is high. Many part-time workers we know are sure they are more productive than their hours would signify simply because they are not so tired or stressed. The battle is to convince their workmates to feel comfortable with their status. Instead of part-time or casual work becoming an option to suit the employee's need to weave together work and other parts of life, many organisations are using casual and part-time jobs to cut their costs. This reinforces the notion that part-time runs a poor second place to full-time work.

Academic Barbara Pocock provides a similarly pessimistic assessment of the status of part-time work and the trade-offs made by those who voluntarily choose not to work full-time. Many part-time jobs in Australia have poor entitlements and are insecure, she points out.[1]

For many in the labour force working part-time is not a choice. Recent studies of flexible work in Australia show the rate of casual employment is growing. ACIRRT, a research and training organisation that monitors and analyses the nature of work, found in a study that 61 per cent of workers in the Australian workforce are now engaged as permanent employees and around one quarter of the workforce is casual.[2] The net increase in jobs in the 1990s consisted almost entirely of casual and part-time jobs.

Yet the voluntary part-time model can work very well with adequate support. Reduced hours can mean reduced stress, less concern about office politics and more time for family. Research backs this anecdotal evidence. US economist Alec Levenson's study of figures over several decades found that four out of five Americans who work less than 35 hours a week 'do so because they do not want full-time work. They want work to fit around their family commitments.'[3] The lack of status part-time work carries could be redressed if more employees opted for this track. In organisations where voluntary part-time work is more common, the status issues often wear away. Options for reduced hours in professional jobs exist in a small but growing number of organisations, including some legal and publishing firms. Even partners at law firms have managed to switch to part-time. Much is made of these cases because they continue to be the exception. Most of the success stories still come from senior employees who are able to negotiate a decent part-time job because their expertise is of such value to their employer. A partner in a Sydney legal firm tells us her switch to part-time hours has helped to streamline her work. Instead of dealing with a range of clients she can focus on a major client, and their relationship has improved, not deteriorated. The day she no longer spends in the office is often used to help at her children's primary school. In such cases, however, part-time work remains a reward rather than a serious career option.

It's not easy, either, to find a part-time job through normal channels, a PR consultant tells us. She spent months looking for a three- or four-day-a-week job and in the end gave up. Her only option, she believed, was to take a full-time role and see if she could eventually reduce her hours when she had proved her worth to her employer. Having taken a full-time role, she now believes it will be impossible to extract herself from a five-day week. In a way, she has performed too well and her colleagues and managers rely on her to be available at all times. She fears that even if she were to cut back to a four-day week her 'day off' would be spent answering calls and queries, thereby defeating the purpose.

It's not too hard to recognise the organisational concern about part-time work, which does more than reduce hours spent in the office or serving customers. Part-time work is unpopular because it can effectively cut the physical and psychological hold of the workplace. Elaborate programs to get commitment are usually redundant for the content part-time worker because they don't need it as a lever to get them to work; their priorities change and their identity is not as dependent on work. They often discover a new way of looking at the job and their absence from the office obviously means less exposure to the corporate message. Work is still alluring but part-time workers can often find a greater sense of autonomy and more space for a personal life. This can sometimes be the case for full-time workers too.

Part-time work is challenging because it cuts to the heart of organisational control. It effectively pulls apart the abiding notion in many offices that long hours are essential to do a good job and that you have to give your all to the workplace.

Significantly, the growing debate around part-time work and commitment runs in parallel with further investment in programs to extract more enthusiasm from staff, particularly in the service sector. In the past few years a swag of books and theories circulated about getting employees to buy in to the project of work. Sometimes we've scoffed at the 'up and at 'em' attitudes implicit here. Sometimes, though, we've seen organisations successfully exploit that approach. When Richard Branson launched his discount airline in Australia, Virgin Blue, the small core of staff working on the start-up talked about being in 'volunteer' mode. Yes, they were getting paid on the flight deck, but in the spirit of the new deal, Virgin Blue wanted them to opt in and choose work, choose life, be *totally there*, every day. Paid volunteers, committed to the cause and doing it for love, meaning and other intangible rewards. At Virgin Blue even the managers take a turn at baggage handling every so often just to show they are part of the team. From the first day of operation the level of commitment was so high it couldn't be manufactured. Virgin Blue's head of Human Resources, Bruce Highfield, told us about the extraordinary atmosphere of the early days. Employees were relating to each other and customers as they would to friends or family, he said, and the enthusiasm was palpable.[4] It didn't hurt to have a charismatic leader like Branson (or Virgin's established reputation as a great employer), nor to occupy the role of David while tackling the Goliath of established domestic airline Qantas. But whatever the ingredients, if Virgin Blue could have bottled the result it would have made a fortune selling it. Management was quick to make the most of the energy and excitement of the early days and has tried to keep the momentum going as the airline grows.

The *Oxford English Dictionary* defines voluntary as a feeling or sentiment 'arising or developing in the mind without external constraint, purely spontaneous in origin or character'. 'Volunteerism' is now being used in the workplace to describe an attitude of having options and the power to decide how to operate at work. The sub-text is that your boss wants to replace the traditional, paternalistic model of employment with a volunteer model 'in which the interests of both the individual and the organisation have to be met and commitment to work, which once could perhaps be assumed, has now to be negotiated and bargained for'.[5] In practice, volunteerism is about the attitude that employees bring to their jobs, the concept of being engaged and enthusiastic, of having absorbed the goals and values of the organisation. The idea is that they have struck a deal about how far they will go in terms of their involvement with the job and the organisation. They have put their hands up for the task.

The volunteer model, Highfield says, is about understanding where a new generation of workers is coming from and involves giving it recognition and trust. It's been crucial for a start-up that needed to generate strong commitment quickly and capitalise on the entrepreneurial style of Branson. Asking people to be volunteers suggests they take a different attitude to their job. The enthusiasm of the volunteer is obviously a key part of the concept because it is an essential component of the Virgin Blue 'offer', the point of difference in a mature and saturated market. Price cutting can attract some custom but for a viable future the airline needs to find ways of connecting the Virgin experience with the flavour of the brand – young, hip and unpretentious. That was not hard when the airline launched, with a small group of dedicated workers, keen to prove they could survive and were willing to buy into the values. As Virgin Blue expands and matures as a public company it's a much bigger ask to get the workforce into volunteer mode.

On the surface, the idea of a new relationship of equal power at work is attractive. It fits perfectly into contemporary ideas that we are a 'brand of one', creating our destiny. We live in a fluid cultural zone, defining ourselves as free agents who exercise choice in every aspect of our lives, from love and marriage to which brand of balsamic vinegar we buy at the supermarket.

Seeing yourself as a volunteer to the project on a daily basis is very different from reporting to work to be told what to do. Volunteering means that you are working for yourself without actually having to run your own business. Volunteer workers are putting in the effort at work, but they see themselves as accruing skills or experiences they can use with another employer or in their personal lives. Work becomes, in part, a personal exercise, and an employee gets more than the pay slip. As the individual discovers more power through work, the job often becomes more controllable and appealing than the rest of life.

Volunteerism is, in some ways, an update of the corporate buzzword of the 1980s – empowerment. Empowerment, says leadership and ethics academic Joanne Ciulla, became a popular term after companies sliced layers of hierarchy away and needed fewer workers to do more. Although it was often tied to the idea that each worker could show leadership and reach for autonomy, empowerment often meant employees doing more work, and feeling they had more power when that was not really the case.[6]

For corporations, volunteerism is also a way of talking about loyalty – an idea that was severely dented in the 1980s and 1990s as job security disappeared. In the past, loyalty to the boss was expected and granted as a matter of course. It was part of the job. But loyalty was a two-way street and assumed employees received something in return for their dedication to the company. Loyalty was about a linear career; it was about staying with the same employer for a lifetime. For the employer loyalty meant holding on to staff who would go the extra mile in return. Volunteerism implies no such deal.

It is an important element of the way some corporations colonise their employees and lock them into the goals of the organisation. The same principle is behind the team-building exercises that pervade large organisations. The elaborate attempts to inculcate a set of common corporate 'team' values at seminars and workshops should not simply be laughed at, silly as they often are. These efforts are so emblematic of big business they have entered popular culture. When Dennis Mitchell, one of the main characters in Elliot Perlman's novel *Seven Types of Ambiguity*, is seriously injured falling from a rope during a team-building exercise, he is furious. His anger is about letting himself be part of an exercise in which he must jettison his own critical faculties and learn to depend on the group, at the bidding of sinister 'therapist' and guru Terry Brabet. Brabet tells the participants, who are meant to be flattered to have been chosen, that he will help them find their true selves by taking them outside their comfort zone.

'He had us all outside again for what he called a "trust" exercise. He tended to volunteer some pseudo social-scientific mumbo jumbo before every session . . . The "trust" exercise, as he called it, was meant to demonstrate that, whatever the undertaking if you had a united team backing you up you had nothing to fear. Something trite like that. Something people want to believe, and that isn't true.'[7]

After he falls and fractures his back, Mitchell reflects: 'Brabet was wrong about it being an exercise in trust. It was an exercise in a man's capacity to clear his mind, even if only momentarily, of all reason and judgment.'[8]

Commitment has always been an important part of the job's contract. Even when scientific management was at its peak, companies could not function without some level of involvement on the part of workers. Humans are not, after all, automatons. But modern companies worry about the level of commitment from employees, largely because of the growth of the service sector. Uncommitted workers can do a lot of damage to a company's brand power. In a recent newspaper survey about customer service at Australia's biggest airline, Qantas, one piece of feedback highlights this point. Flight-deck staff had been grumpy and uninterested in giving any real service on a recent flight. The respondent didn't blame them – rather, he recognised that Qantas staff had been pushed to anger by the management's approach to industrial relations. It wasn't surprising then that they were not putting in much effort with customers.[9] This man registered a negative response for Qantas, not for the staff. There's always a danger that disgruntled employees will send the wrong signals at a time when customers are so fickle. This is why so many corporations now talk about making sure their employees act as ambassadors for the company at all times, in and out of work hours. It's part of the deal in the era of 'emotional labour' where employees are expected to invest as much in their attitude reinforcement as their skills training.

Volunteerism works well in organisations like Virgin Blue but companies with more traditional workplaces and operations need different ways to make employees 'get with the program'. Sometimes organisations use formal systems to monitor employees' interactions with customers, including good old-fashioned surveillance. What companies are confronting here are the intangibles of employees' attitudes. The larger the organisation, the more difficult it is to ensure your ambassadors are giving the right messages to customers. An entire call centre industry now takes it for granted that listening in on your employees as they handle customers is a natural part of the work contract.

It seemed to us quite shocking to hear about the Commonwealth Bank's attempts to monitor branch staff through a technique called 'mystery shopping'. Although it has since been modified after complaints from the staff, customers and the union, the process involved sending disguised 'shoppers' into the branches to check if the tellers were following a script when dealing with customers. Staff were penalised if, for example, they failed to use the customer's name, to thank them or to cross-sell products. Enough failures and the staff were placed on the bank's 'managing unacceptable performance' program.[10] Concern about mystery shopping is understandable: it's an extreme example of the attempt to control attitude. It's also not hard to understand why these techniques are being trialed, given the pressure on large banks to convert into customer service organisations. These formal levels of monitoring and measuring are not available or allowable in all organisations. Instead, psychological levers including volunteerism, commitment, empowerment and authenticity are used to get a positive attitude from employees.

Getting the most out of the hearts and minds of workers will continue to be a big issue for what some commentators have termed the 'attention economy'. The notion that much of the world of service is about giving attention or paying attention emerges in books published in the past few years by two of the most interesting American thinkers on work and society. Thomas Davenport, a consultant and academic, argues that attention is the new currency of business.[11] As products become cheaper and more abundant, business people have a problem: how to get and hold the attention of consumers, stockholders and potential employees. Robert Reich, in his book *The Future of Success*, notes the extent to which so much of the economy is about paying for attention – whether from an upmarket sales assistant, a personal coach, a nanny or a financial adviser.

'What's also being bought and sold is a relationship,' says

Reich. 'The easy familiarity with which your personal trainer greets you, the friendship of a massage therapist, the little confidences shared with your Rolfer [deep massage therapist] or even the person who parks your car.'[12] Spin that out to the many dozens of encounters we all have every day with people whose *employers* we are paying for attention, and it's clear why companies need staff to engage in new ways. The emphasis on a 'quality' experience with staff is possibly greater now when there are fewer people to serve customers and banks are busy promoting internet services or automatic tellers. There are fewer face-to-face encounters but those who remain in direct contact with customers are carrying a heavier burden of care and they must invest more emotional labour than ever.

The attitudes of workers and their emotional commitment can often reflect the mores of their generation. Researchers believe Generation X (born between 1960 and 1980) and Generation Next (1980 on) are very different from the Veterans (1922 to 1943) and Baby Boomers (1943 to 1960).[13]

The general idea is that Veterans are hardworking individualists; Baby Boomers are hardworking team players; Xers are aggressively individualistic and work even harder still; while Nexters are more likely to work with the group but want more balance in their lives. It's the last group, the Nexters and those just a little older, who are the real target for 'volunteerism'. James Hall, a twenty-three-year-old journalist, tells us, 'The Xers were single-mindedly focused on careers and staying with careers but we see ourselves moving in and out of work, putting together the package more flexibly.'[14]

That mix is clearly emerging in the way young people juggle work and study. Very few students just go to university anymore. Even those enrolled full-time often include a hefty dose of work in their programs, so more and more we will see young people with one foot in the workplace and one out. They will not want work or study to stop them from enjoying other experiences like travel, or working overseas for the joy of it, rather than for career advancement. Many in Australia will be forced to blend study and work to pay for their tuition and postpone the travel. The challenge will be to see whether they can retain that flexibility or whether the financial demands of graduate study, plus partnering and babies, will restrict them as such life-changes have restricted previous generations. But if Zygmunt Bauman is right about the liquid world we live in, where we keep the bonds loose and flexible, it may be that the Nexters will partner and procreate less and less, a move which will surely make them less geographically tied and harder to hold in jobs.

Again, our Nexter colleague James Hall sums up the generation's approach to work: 'We're not necessarily passionate about our work but we don't see it as separate from life. In a sense, work is about someone sponsoring you to live – it's like a paid vocation.'[15] Vocation is a very old-fashioned word for a modern workplace and some analysts see the concept re-emerging at a time when work has become so consuming that there are few other spaces where we can test our identity.

Employability is another relatively new idea in this field of worker attitude. Here the individual is encouraged to see themself as developing a suite of skills and experience that makes them a good 'buy' for the boss. The emphasis is on giving power back to the worker but it is up to the individual worker to make sure they are employable. This idea emerged after the big economic changes in the 1980s and 1990s when employers were relieved of any long-term responsibility for retaining staff. It also disguises the economic reality that jobs are often unavailable. And employability is often used to make 'bogus promises' to compensate for the insecurity of jobs, writes Joanne Ciulla in her book *The Working*

Life.[16] In reality, the training for one job is unlikely to be an exact match for another role, or it may have become obsolete. When it works, however, employability is an attractive notion because it offers the prospect of control, something that complements the love affair with work.

In contrast, workers of previous generations felt tied to the company and not to a set of skills: a consultant working with retrenched executives tells us some of the people he talks to are unable to really detach themselves from their former organisation and see their skills as quite specific to a particular job. Robert Reich writes of the period before technology really kicked in the 1970s. Back then, we had an economy based on large-scale, standardised production where jobs were 'co-ordinated like clockwork'.[17] These large, bureaucratic organisations promised stable, if sometimes tedious, work for which people were rewarded based on the time spent at the task, rather than the outcome. The trade-off for the tedium was predictability, stability and, very often, some sort of union protection which was accepted by the bosses as well as the workers. But our futures are now about innovation, flexibility and rapid responses to global competition and market demands. It's a 'Jack be nimble, Jack be quick' kind of world. Volunteerism is about getting on the bus quickly, or being left behind. And like employability, it is a notion that works best for the privileged workers at the top of the work pole. For many others, left to mop up with the less glamorous, badly paid and tedious work, employability is purely academic.

Employability puts the focus and responsibility for succeeding in the workplace on the individual, ignoring many of the bigger social and economic issues that leave some people disadvantaged. It also presupposes a workplace where you're expected to shake hands politely and depart when the work dries up. No hard feelings on either side. According to Richard Dunford, an academic at

Macquarie Graduate School of Management, when consultants and companies talk about employability, it is based on the idea that work is a series of transactions between equals. That is, when the merry-go-round stops and the work runs out or when employees leave, there will be mutual acceptance of this. Supposedly no one loses in this 'mature state relationship'. It's a long way from the reality of many sackings and a long way from the fear and loathing created by mass downsizings and re-engineering. In this regard, Dunford believes, there has been something of a turnaround in attitudes by companies since the bad old days of the 1990s. They are moving back to a recognition that holding on to staff, selecting and training them well, is a better approach.[18]

Even so, there will be little choice but for those serious about work to take responsibility for their own careers, even as the commentators argue over whether careers exist. Whatever the title, the notion of developing a portfolio of skills is already taken for granted by Generations X and Next. Any serious teenager is aware of the need for a breadth of work experience on their CV even before they finish high school, and getting the right mix (a summer internship, some junior management experience, a bit of retail) is well-established as a concept by the time they are at university.

Work has changed in the past fifty years and it's true that we have to look at our working lives and careers in different terms. As the attention economy grows, strategies like volunteerism will spread as companies try to entice workers to come on board, preferably full-time, mentally and physically, and help promote the public face of the organisation. The investment in and sophistication of these efforts is about to increase dramatically.

1. Pocock, Barbara. *The Work/Life Collision*. Federation Press, 2003, p.167.
2. 'The Future of Work: Trends and Challenges in Australian Workplaces', Australian Centre of Industrial Relations Research and Training, June 2003.
3. Cited in Ciulla, Joanne. *The Working Life*, Three Rivers Press, 2001, p. 184.
4. 'Best employers', *AFR BOSS*, March 2003.
5. Gratton, Lynda and Sumantra Ghosal. 'Managing personal human capital: new ethos for the "volunteer" employee', *European Management Journal*, Vol. 21, Issue 1, February 2000, pp. 1–10.
6. Ciulla, op cit., p. 135.
7. Perlman, Elliott, *Seven Types of Ambiguity*. Picador, 2003, p. 293.
8. Ibid. p. 294.
9. Reported in *The Sydney Morning Herald*, 29 August 2003, p. 8.
10. Denholm, Matthew. 'Which bank's tellers are shopping mad', *The Mercury*, 10 April 2003, p. 5.
11. Davenport and Beck, op cit.
12. Reich, op cit., p.186.
13. Zemke, Ron et al. *Generations at Work: Managing the Clash of Veterans, Boomers, Xers, and Nexters in Your Workplace*. Amacom, 2000, p. 3.
14. Interview with James Hall.
15. Ibid.
16. Ciulla, op cit., p. 232.
17. Reich, op cit., p. 95.
18. Interview with Richard Dunford.

7

Designer workers: measuring behaviour in the office

THE BOSS FROM HELL APPEARED in the English TV comedy series *The Office* as David Brent, manager of Wernham-Hogg Paper Merchants, Slough. The internet site for the comedy describes him as 'a true Renaissance Man for the twenty-first century. He is an accomplished dancer, poet, philosopher, satirist, and perhaps most impressively for these times, football player.'[1]

In fact, he is none of these things, but he is a supremely poor judge of character and a clumsy oaf when he interacts with his staff. The dialogue in *The Office* is often muted, even monosyllabic. It's what isn't said that makes the excruciating comedy about modern office behaviour so devastatingly funny and depressing. All of us have worked in that kind of office where we've exchanged knowing glances with colleagues and shrivelled with embarrassment or disgust at the shenanigans.

At times *The Office* is hard to watch. It's far too close to reality. That could explain why relatively few offices appear in popular culture.

We work in an office ourselves, in what is best described as a dynamic environment, which provides another layer of first-hand experience to the theory regularly crossing our desks. And we are frequently approached by companies and consultants keen to tell us about their latest breakthrough or approach. In the past couple of years this wave of information has taken a new turn with many organisations investing big money in programs concentrating on the behaviour of workers and the culture of their workspace. These companies want workers to devote more of their time to work and are trying to tap into the passion and dedication that some employees have for their jobs. They want to find the key to turning their people on to the idea of work being satisfying and fulfilling: and inducing them to work even harder.

This is a fascinating trend because, superficially, it flies in the face of decades of dry dogma about the bottom line. Even when the dot com boom spawned a new framework, casual and driven by mind-blowing ideas, the emphasis was on the results. Wearing jeans to work and having free-form meetings was fine, as long as there was a spike in the share price. Now the talk is about soft skills, emotions and behaviour. But the underlying focus remains on productivity and results.

As *The Office* reveals, many of us have a set of behaviours that belong to the office and not other parts of life. Meeting a feared manager in a social setting can often reinforce this dichotomy. That pleasant and amusing person may bear little resemblance to the curt, authoritarian executive at the office who is only interested in the next deadline. That's because how we behave at work makes a difference to how much we produce. It's hardly a recent discovery. The benefit of harnessing organisational behaviour to boost productivity was identified a century ago. Analysing how to change behaviour and get everyone on the 'right' path rapidly became a major twentieth-century business preoccupation.

These days it's all a bit more sophisticated. No more crude references to fitting a square peg into a round hole: the latest talk is about motivation, attitude and emotional intelligence. That's the so-called soft skill set. More hard-edged is the focus on measuring people-related areas. Human Resources practices, such as recruitment procedures, staff retention, training and development investment and even attitudes and behaviour are all being 'quantified'. The process is aimed at calculating the value of employees. After decades of only viewing employees as a cost through the wages bill, the measurement of human capital, or HC, allows people to be seen as 'value drivers' – the capital, assets or services that are instrumental to the company making profits – and therefore as business assets. It's moving people from the debit to the credit side of the ledger.

That sounds like a step forward and in some ways it is. Focusing on the employees and the systems to support them appears to be a welcome change from the depersonalised rhetoric about the bottom line. It reflects a new way of thinking about the organisation and the role of business as a community of people. At that level it is a very modern idea that fits in with the thinking of groups such as the cultural creatives. But forcing these intangible elements into a financial framework is also fraught with danger.

Measurement is not a benign or neutral process. At its most cynical, measurement of some aspects of human capital is attempting to put value on something that does not belong to the organisation: the very nature of the people employed. At the same time, attempts to identify and reinforce the 'right' behaviour and the 'best' culture are a way of seeking to control and mould workplace attitudes. These processes, including psychological testing, questionnaires and employee assessments, are even at risk of reinforcing 'designer employees' who will behave and think in the right ways to fall in line with marketplace requirements. These tactics are part of the organisational bid to bind us ever more closely to the workplace, and they feed an addiction to our jobs as they seek to tie more and more of our personality to our work.

Today, there is little questioning of the right of the organisation to try to value or align the heads, bodies and even hearts of workers. This is an immense leap from the traditional idea of the employee who turned up, worked and left at the end of the day. And it's another reminder of the impact the workplace has on every facet of life – there are few areas that are off-limits to the organisation now. Giving up weekends to attend training or working until midnight to finish a project is simply par for the course for many employees.

At the same time, the idea that a business is not simply an economic entity but a powerful part of society has gained support. It was pressure from those advocating this reassessment that sparked a new wave of measurement.

We've been intrigued to see another level of measurement become the approach 'du jour' for large companies around Australia. The culture change program is coming to a workplace near you. But don't expect much straight-talking about what it means or the real aims of these hugely expensive exercises. The rhetoric is all about cultural transformation and revitalisation of values, along with new mission statements. Despite being issued in management-speak about 'soft' skills and behaviour, many of these efforts have some clear efficiency goals. We have sat through a lot of briefings on culture change programs in the last few years. We've heard about 'getting on the balcony' at the National Australia Bank (that's when participants get the bigger picture about what is happening in the organisation – they are able to stand above the fray and observe what is changing) and heard the definition of 'pity city' at Qantas (a metaphor for the whinging veterans who want to talk about how much better the workplace was in the old days). It's hard not to be amused, wary and then sceptical of the corporate-speak and huge investment in some of these efforts. Many of these programs are part of another wave of corporate attempts to align employees' behaviour at work with productivity goals.

It would be a mistake to dismiss these efforts as merely tinkering, given the investment made by companies. What has struck us is the consistent and ambitious goal of reshaping the very attitudes of employees to the organisation and their work and to encourage them to conform to a prescribed set of behaviours. The paradox is that these programs are usually couched as an alternative to a rigid approach to work, which will encourage diversity and creativity. Our research shows that the overall effect of the culture makeover is often the exact opposite. In Australia, all four retail banks have now announced multi-million-dollar cultural transformation plans. Other large organisations, such as BHP, Woodside, Qantas and even investment bank ABN AMRO, have joined the move.

At the NAB a team of enthusiastic people sat around a table to brief us on the way their cultural reform program, called Breakthrough, was progressing. As we reported in *AFR Boss* in April 2003, the team assured us it was not a 'thinly disguised productivity exercise nor a series of touchy feely hugging sessions'. The senior ranks were mostly 'on board' and the idea was to change the culture of the bank. The program was made up of a series of workshops and employees could 'volunteer' to attend.

Breakthrough was one part of a broader range of activities taking place in the bank under the title Revitalisation. They were all designed to address a range of concerns about the culture and operations of the NAB that had been identified in a series of surveys and research work. Traditionally, the bank had a strong process orientation, explained Karen Noble, global manager, innovation and quality at the NAB. Breakthrough, she explained, aimed to transform the bank into a more modern and flexible financial institution.[2]

At the briefing senior NAB executive Wayne Rees, general manager of financial services, NSW, said a program was needed to help change the old-fashioned, paternal style of the bank. Staff looked to head office for the answers, but management don't always have the solutions. The NAB was an enormous place and trying to find your way through it is not easy. 'This is about how you change a culture so that everyone has ownership,' Rees said.[3]

With the cultural reform program had come a whole new way of speaking, Karen Noble explained, which was spreading throughout the bank and was a sign the program was working. It was, the team stressed, all about changing behaviour (which they called the soft stuff) to get better bottom line results (the hard). 'We couldn't communicate about the hard issues without the soft,' Noble said. 'We had to approach the soft stuff. Now we are tapping into mindsets and behaviours to get cultural change. This revolves around trust, transparency, and accountability and empowerment.'[4]

And it was working, the team said. Even then CEO Frank Cicutto featured in a video of a Breakthrough workshop, applauding employees. Put simply, it aimed to improve employees' relationships with customers and to get more ideas from them about improvements.

In 2004 the NAB has been through a major upheaval with CEO Frank Cicutto resigning. The new CEO, John Stewart, immediately targeted the bank's culture as a priority for his attention.

A few months after our NAB briefing in 2003, in another CBD office a group of consultants and managers working with or for the Qantas engineering division, which employs more than 6,000 people, outlined an elaborate organisational renewal process they were in the middle of 'rolling out'.[5] The division includes a number of troubled workplaces, splintered by industrial unrest and a series of redundancies, and the new model, illustrated by charts and drawings, suggests new ways of talking about work processes, jobs and reporting lines. Once again there's a language peculiar to the process. One of the key reasons it was needed, says one of the consultants, is that the management were not communicating well enough with employees. A major cultural program was seen as the solution.

These culture change processes, usually presented to the financial market as a 'phase' in the growth of the business, have many consequences. Some bosses are well aware of the dangers of labelling any initiative in the office as a 'change' program. Management academic Richard Dunford remembers working with a company in the 1980s around the time of the introduction of the Japanese-inspired 'quality circles', a concept designed to improve process and products. Don't, begged the general manager, call them 'quality circles'. We're running discussion groups about doing things differently but if you label it, it won't work, he told Dunford. Dunford argues strongly that behaviour is what shapes values, not the other way around.[6]

When the organisation cannot recognise this, it imposes a group of values which often have little to do with reality or are so general they lose meaning. This is often summarised as a mission statement – a creature so ubiquitous that few employees would be unfamiliar with the term. As Don Watson wrote in *Death Sentence*, the mission statement is usually so banal it has little meaning and becomes interchangeable among organisations. The same kinds of values are set out in the mission statements of the CIA and McDonald's, he points out. For many employees, the corporate mission statement printed on brochures or laminated wallet-sized cards can provoke deep unease, if not cynicism.[7]

At our briefing at the NAB one of the team handed us a

business card. On the back was printed a mission statement:

At the National we value:

Service to our customers;

Quality in everything we do;

Competitiveness and a will to win;

Growing profit for our stakeholders;

Continuous productivity improvement;

Growth and development of our people;

Professionalism and ethics in all our actions.

Mission statements certainly get a mixed reception. A senior manager at a large professional services firm told us: 'I hate the mission statement all over our brochures and business cards, and blaring out from our ads. It's just at odds with how the organisation operates, and the way employees are treated. It's become an in joke around here. People sarcastically quote it when something awful happens or another area gets closed down.'

We have visited dozens of workplaces and found walls behind reception desks and in conference rooms plastered with some kind of mission statement. At Vodafone Australia's Sydney head office, brightly coloured posters and friezes cover the walls with pictures of smiling faces interwoven with words like 'fun'.

But work often doesn't seem much like fun. These words are not just bland, they don't have a lot to do with how it feels to be at work. The boss of a beverage company told us about the need to use a new mission statement to help involve the many employees at the company who were not interested in drinking alcohol and who felt disenfranchised from the core business. He said that by focusing on sociability, rather than the alcohol itself, there would be more 'buy-in' from employees. These statements of values are not confined to commercial corporations. When a suburban public school spends six months developing a mission statement, it is clear that the trend to package up 'core values' is widespread. The need to codify and simplify quite complex elements of behaviour in organisations is a strong factor in the popularity of these slogans. The thinking appears to be that by registering the ideals, behaviour will then fall into line, deeply etched into employees' psyches.

No matter how simplistic the rhetoric about a new culture or set of values, there is usually a lot of effort invested in cultural change programs. Author and academic Dr John Garrett believes that the effects these patterns have on the way in which people are required to behave at work and how their workplace attitudes are moulded as a consequence have not been adequately considered. Underpinning this trend to analyse and redefine this amorphous concept of 'corporate culture' is productivity. And, as Garrett points out, that triggers a lot of really big questions about the subtlety and seductiveness of the social engineering that goes with it. Many employees buy into 'cultural change' because they are being rewarded for it financially or with a promotion. But their hearts are not in it.

By defining the 'right' organisational behaviour there is an increased risk of prescriptive practices and recruitment. That's a path which ultimately benefits neither the employee nor the business. 'At the end of the day there is something to the idea of having a team that is really functioning well because of its coherence, as distinct from a team that doesn't work well,' says Garrett. 'You will get more rewards from working hard, is the message, but there's a religiosity of the theme. It's very materialistic and mechanistic.'[8]

Ralph Stacey is professor of management and director of the Complexity and Management Centre at the Business School of the University of Hertfordshire in the UK. He believes that the growth of culture change programs is based on the false assumption that people are automatons. This mechanistic engineering model assumes the outcome of human behaviour can be predicted, which is absurd, he points out. Most workers do not simply do what they are told at all times, but many sophisticated culture change programs continue to operate on this premise. The move to get everyone aligned with the common good, the agreed 'culture' or with the 'team', is aided by the focus on measurement, where standards of 'professional' behaviour are mapped and reinforced.[9]

All this effort is not simply about the value people add to business. It can also include identifying the best contributors and the patterns of behaviour that produce better results so they can be replicated. If the organisation can identify the 'right' aptitude and behaviour for certain jobs then it's possible to feed that straight through to the recruitment process. Any trawl through the job advertisements will show this is already happening – often with the aid of psychometric testing.

The controversial and short-lived head of the Australian Broadcasting Corporation, Jonathon Shier, became notorious for his management style and, in particular, his love of psychometric testing. During a flurry of restructuring, he had one of his senior and most experienced executives, Hugh McGowan, sit for a series of tests in order to take on a new position. Annoyed at the request, and by questions such as 'Do you lie?', McGowan resigned. The McGowan affair was leaked to the media and sparked a heated debate about Shier's tactics and his faith in psychometric testing. Critics attacked the concept that certain personality and intelligence results could determine the suitability of candidates for a job. Just as vehemently, psychometric testers defended their patch, maintaining the use of tests is simply a more efficient and fair way of pinpointing people for particular jobs. About thirty per cent of Australian companies are estimated to use these testing tools regularly, either for external appointments or internal promotions. Once used mainly for management ranks, some companies are now using testing from the factory floor up. Australians generally tend to resist this idea of pigeonholing people according to test results. It doesn't sit well with our ideal of fair play and giving everyone a go. But its use is quietly growing. Leading investment bank Macquarie Bank, for example, has used psychometric testing for years to help select employees. Getting a job, it seems, is no longer about what you can do but how you go about it and how you behave, particularly in Australia where the economy no longer revolves around production but around services.

Even Human Resources professionals get worried about the overuse of testing in recruitment. The head of HR for a large services organisation told us she was ever more wary of psychometric results being given too much weight in determining suitability for a job. A number of freshly graduated MBAs she knew had found their failure to get jobs was solely the result of such tests. While not advocating dropping testing altogether, she believed it had to be used very carefully and as part of a suite of tools to assess candidates for jobs or promotions.

This game of matching people to workplaces has become more and more refined, despite continuing criticism about the dangers of pigeonholing people, the potential for faking responses and the inability of tests to predict future behaviour. Fans of the psychometric test claim it must be better than the flawed process of interviewing and using a CV to assess a candidate. But testing also provides numbers to rely on rather than intuition. It offers an insurance policy for managers worried about hiring a non-player, and it allows a depersonalised process to replace what has always been a human interaction, flawed as it may be.

Psychometric testing is just part of a range of measurement tools. Some elements of this trend are linked to the wave of interest in valuing 'intangibles', such as brand value and knowledge, which has swept through organisational thinking. Coca-Cola and News Limited led the charge in calculating the value of their high profile brands or mastheads so they could be added to the bottom line. Intangibles came to include the human dimension of business – the knowledge and skills brought to and practised in the business by employees. It's recognition to be welcomed: if the value of people is taken more seriously, then presumably there is more reason to treat employees fairly and nurture individual talent.

Valuing knowledge is a tricky proposition, however, and has resulted in some core questions about ownership of intellectual capital (IC). In recent years, some ad agencies have tussled with their clients over who owns the ideas behind a successful campaign. Is it the client, who pays for the agency to come up with the campaign in the first place, or the creatives at the agency? Intellectual capital is fast becoming an issue for the decade as universities and biotech firms alike attempt to set up a framework for the future. With so much value tied up in the brain power of employees, the emphasis on valuing knowledge seems logical. Unfortunately the methods to do so are often limited in scope or difficult to fit into traditional accounting frameworks.

This trend to instil more measurement in previously uncharted waters is not confined to the private sector. It's becoming even more popular in the public sector. It is not going unchecked, however, with critics blaming the obsession on bureaucracy gone mad, and even accusing it of subverting the operation of institutions such as the law. In a speech in late 2001, the Chief Justice of New South Wales, Jim Spigelman, told a Sydney audience of his concern with the inappropriate use of quantitative measurement in the administration of justice. Measurement, he said, was often painted as a rational and objective means to enhance efficiency. But this is usually not the case.

'There is a tendency amongst managers to regard measurement as benign and that no harm can be done from quantification even

Designer workers: measuring behaviour in the office

if it does not prove useful. That is wrong. The process of deciding what and how to measure so-called "performance" is capable of having very real effects on behaviour and of distorting actual conduct in a manner that no one would actually choose. This is a critical manifestation of the irrationality of partial rationality.'[10]

Performance indicators, he pointed out, often have perverse effects, particularly when they influence resource allocation and job security or remuneration. Measurement is not neutral and it has repercussions. 'Distortion arises because the things that can be measured are not the only things that matter,' he said.[11] His comments made quite an impression on the audience that evening, many of whom were completing a course in leadership run by an Australian charity, the Benevolent Society. While measurement in the recruitment arena may well help to match the person to the job and thus bind some employees even more firmly to the workplace, it has some significant flaws, as Spigelman points out, and should be used with care. People are different from other company assets.

Enthusiasm for measurement of employees, however, is stronger than ever. When one of us interviewed English author and consultant Alexander Mayo about the use of measurement, he was sure the wave of interest in the latest techniques was filtering through to the accountancy profession in the United Kingdom.[12] It's a new idea in an otherwise fairly static accounting environment. Quantitative models for measuring the impact of people on the bottom line are proliferating. Mayo has devised a 'human capital monitor' which concentrates on measuring areas such as the costs of employment (including recruitment and replacement costs), reward systems and motivation levels through employee surveys, and broader signals from analysing the contribution by IC to the company's value. These are then tallied and included in the traditional financial statements that end up in the annual report.

145

But how is it possible to measure how someone behaves? In the workplace, measurement in this context usually means a framework for ranking the skills of employees, along with their attitudes and behaviour. Some assessment is usually made of performance (completed projects, customer satisfaction and so on) and information collected through 360-degree feedback. This is a controversial tool to assess employees by gathering information from a range of colleagues: senior, junior and peers. Those asked to provide information may feel they have extra power and a chance to make a contribution to the way the workplace operates. But there have been many problems with 360-degree assessments. Junior staff fear reprisals if they give an honest opinion; the information garnered may simply be ignored or it is too sensitive and can be destructive if used. As with other forms of people measurement, 360-degree feedback often reinforces certain behaviour since despite the corporate talk about diversity and flexibility, many companies have a fairly narrow definition of how they wish employees to behave at work.

At its heart, measurement is always about efficiency and that's what the system, and indeed the market economy, is all about. Gradually, the notion that the control or reinforcement of certain behaviour is desirable and possible is seeping into the thinking about work. Every time a performance review is carried out a manager is reinforcing the 'right' behaviour for the job, and every knowledge management or creativity session seeks to pin down or codify processes to help the company avoid the risk of losing intellectual property.

While enjoying a resurgence in popularity, this need to put numbers around the people in the organisation in an attempt to replicate success and weed out failure is not a new phenomenon in business. It was the motivating force behind experiments conducted by scientific management expert Frederick Winslow

Taylor in US factories such as Ford in the early years of last century, and later the infamous Hawthorne experiments conducted by George Elton Mayo in Western Electric's Hawthorne Works in Chicago.

Although well known within the management world, the lessons from the Hawthorne experiments are worthy of a far wider airing. In the 1920s, identifying the triggers to greater productivity in the workplace was just beginning to provoke the interest of managers and business owners. The Hawthorne studies were a series of experiments on groups of factory workers aimed at finding if changes in physical conditions would boost output. One part of the research involved using different intensity of lighting to see if employees worked harder. At first this did seem to be the case. Vary the lighting and productivity went up. Over time the effect diminished and the researchers eventually concluded that the attention from those conducting the study, combined with less direct supervision and more emphasis on teamwork, were the reasons for increased work rates.[13]

The 'Hawthorne effect' is still used to describe the improvement in work quality that comes from increased attention to and investment in people factors rather than other elements of the workspace. The measurement craze picks up on the same theme but with a more ambitious agenda. This latest attempt doesn't stop at setting up a range of optimal conditions for workers but actually seeks to find the most effective behavioural triggers.

It is crossing a line for some early pioneers of human capital measurement, who have come to warn of the pitfalls of measurement. Jeffrey Pfeffer, professor of organisational behaviour at Stanford University, told *Fast Company* that 'measurement has become a tyranny that makes sure that nothing gets done'.[14] And the head of the Australian HR Association, Jo Mithen, recently warned against too much reliance on measurement in the workplace.[15]

The quest to find out how to push our behaviour buttons has moved into even more surprising realms in recent times. At *AFR BOSS*, we have run articles about evolutionary psychology and even articles on how bird watching can be useful in the business world, as animal behaviour tells management a lot about human patterns.[16] The interest in the measurement of human capital is running parallel with these efforts to understand why we behave the way we do at work. It's not unusual to pick up a management journal and read about a disparate blend of sociology and behavioural science, as the quest for more information on work behaviour broadens.

Who would have thought Charles Darwin would make it into management books? Evolutionary Psychology (EP) contends that we are born with certain facets of human behaviour hardwired into our brains, just like black hair or green eyes. The brain hasn't had a chance to change much because adaptation takes thousands of years and we are a relatively recently evolved species, still carrying Stone Age behaviour triggers in our heads. While EP is not a system of measurement it can nevertheless be used in business as a tool to recognise patterns of behaviour. Nigel Nicholson, a London Business School academic, wrote a book on the topic that sparked much debate on how far and how prescriptive the study of human behaviour at work should be. Executives, he tells us, lap it up.[17]

Measuring the human dimension of business, either in its broadest sense as a community or more specifically, is becoming a corporate tool for change. After all, people and the way they do their work is the new capital. But, as British management thinker Charles Handy says, you may put a price on intangibles but you can't own them: 'It is no longer sensible, perhaps not even moral, for the financiers to claim that they can own the skills or the experience of the people in the business. This sort of intangible property can only belong to the individuals who have those skills and experience.'[18] And this is a crucial distinction. What you think belongs to you and you know it. You own your ideas and the way you think.

Imposing or reinforcing standards of behaviour or cultural norms is often an exercise in control. At a time when the talk from the top of organisations is all about the individual, creativity and autonomy, a wave of measurement tools is reinforcing a narrow set of norms. This culture change fad is ambitious in its claims. It seeks to quantify and replicate human behaviour and it's based on the premise that this is possible and desirable. But it doesn't make sense for many workers, who are suspicious of the motives no matter what their work is or the level of satisfaction they derive from their job.

The human measurement specialists and behaviouralists of the corporate world are not working from sinister or greedy motives. This trend cannot be simply labelled as Orwellian and dismissed. Most of these specialists believe they are doing something positive and critical for workers in modern corporate structures and even providing some employees with better working conditions and a renewed sense of purpose. But most of their efforts are long on blather and they are unfolding within the market system where the drive to extract more from a depleted labour force is unrelenting.

1. From *The Office* website (www.bbc.co.uk/comedy/theoffice/) written by Clare Kneeshaw.
2. Fox, Catherine. 'Workers by design', *AFR BOSS*, August 2003.
3. Fox, Catherine and Cornell, Andrew. 'Too little, too late', *AFR BOSS*, March 2004.
4. Fox, Catherine. 'Workers by design', *AFR BOSS*, August 2003.
5. Interview with Qantas staff.
6. Interview with Richard Dunford.
7. Watson, Don. *Death Sentence: The Decay of Public Language*. Knopf, 2003.
8. Fox, Catherine. 'Workers by design', *AFR BOSS*, August 2003.

9. Ibid.

10. Chief Justice Jim Spigelman. Speech to Sydney Leadership Alumni, Sydney, May 2003.

11. Ibid.

12. Fox, Catherine. 'The challenge of measuring up', *The Australian Financial Review*, 22 October 2002, p. 59.

13. *Business: The Ultimate Resource*. Bloomsbury, *2002*.

14. Cited in Turner, Rebecca. 'Managing by numbers', *AFR BOSS*, February 2003.

15. Fox, Catherine. 'HR is more than being good with people', *The Australian Financial Review*, 29 April 2003, p. 66.

16. Coutu, Diane L. 'Of birds and business', *Harvard Business Review*, June 2002. Reproduced in *AFR BOSS*.

17. Fox, Catherine. 'This man says we're just tribes at work', *AFR BOSS*, June 2002.

18. Handy, Charles. *The Hungry Spirit*. Random House, 1997, p. 161.

8

Can capitalism afford kids?

'THERE'S NOT WORK AND LIFE – there's just life and work is something you do during your life,' IBM executive Janet Perna tells a room full of working women in Sydney.[1] They are gathered to hear how Perna has risen through the ranks to become one of the most senior women in one of the world's biggest companies. Most of the audience nod as they listen, but it's a fair bet they don't feel that work is just a part of life when they hit the office every morning.

At IBM, where Perna has worked for thirty years, there are now special committees and policies to inject some flexibility into a regular working life. It used to be women of child-bearing age who were asking for more flexibility. These days, it's Baby Boomers, Generation Xers and all the others who want to opt out or downshift. Perna has been able to move people into part-time roles, give them sabbaticals or set up new arrangements. It certainly helps to have an open-minded boss – and some similar policies – to keep the hands on deck.

As journalists we are fortunate to have more annual leave than many other professionals. Perhaps that's why the school holidays are so noticeable at our office – the men (and they are usually men) in charge who have school-age children are often all away at the same time. Once their stay-at-home wives did the caring. But how do you run the office when there's no one around? Will the system, with its drive for ever-improving productivity, continue to allow us to have children?

The pernicious relationship between hours at the desk and validity as a worker has proved far tougher to dismantle than anyone thought possible. This is where the addiction to work becomes manifest – the long hours on the job have virtually acted as a contraceptive for a whole generation. Work is replacing not only sex, but reproduction of the species. The birth rate has declined in most developed economies, and women are waiting longer to have children. Average family size has shrunk dramatically. Surveys to uncover why this is so invariably come up with the same kinds of answers: for educated middle-class women there is a choice to be made between a career or breeding.

Europe's population is expected to decrease rapidly as fertility levels fall, a major 2003 study by the Population Reference Bureau found.[2] An increasing focus by many women on education and career and away from child-rearing roles is a major factor in the projected decline, the researchers said. Meanwhile even developing countries are experiencing a decline in fertility in some parts of society which is attributed to a number of factors, including the entry of women into the workforce and increased access to contraception. There are few signs this pattern is temporary – most of the studies on demographic trends suggest further falls.

For young, well-educated women there is overwhelming anecdotal and research evidence supporting the idea that a decision about what to do with your life is between a career (with all the accompanying status and material trappings) and kids. These women have watched their Baby Boomer mothers struggle to do both and there's no way most of them want that fiasco. This squeeze to fit in rearing a family with paid employment has become even tighter with the manic dedication of more and more hours to the job.

It's easy to forget it wasn't always this way. The idea that long hours are a prerequisite for success is a relatively new phenomenon, but one that has caught on hard and fast. Even in countries such as France where a thirty-five-hour work week was legislated at the beginning of 2000, professionals have generally continued to work long hours, particularly if they are employed by a multinational. The viability of the shorter working week, which provoked vehement criticism from countries like the United States (where working long hours is almost a religion) is being questioned within France. Prime Minister Jean-Pierre Raffarin told the French National Assembly in October 2003 that a parliamentary commission was being established to review the effect of the reduced work week on businesses, on the economy and on government finances. Concerns about France's ability to compete have been a continuing theme since the reduced working week was introduced. Cutting standard working hours challenged some aspects of national identity, a former colleague now living in France told us. The connection between hours and a serious attitude to work was reflected in Raffarin's comment when announcing the thirty-five-hour week review: 'Work must be a central value of our society.'[3]

The roots of this obsession can be traced back a hundred years or so. In the first decades of last century the union movement played a major role in pushing for standardised working weeks, which were then legislated in many Western economies. But this framework was eroded gradually. Despite the moves to minimise hours in a number of countries, by the late 1930s and certainly after the Second World War the work hours of many in the West started to increase again, and 'beginning in the late 1960s, the United States entered an era of rising work time'.[4]

Australia is no exception, despite our sentimental national image of a laid-back, relaxed society. Most of us don't need to be told that the average hours of work here are on the increase, at the same time as societal pressure to achieve status and the material trappings of a successful lifestyle are intensifying.[5] In Australia the average working week has increased from forty-two hours to forty-four hours since 1982. About 1.7 million people, roughly thirty per cent of full time employees, work more than fifty hours a week and that's twice as many as two decades ago. Australians work as long as people in any Western country, an Organisation for Economic Co-operation and Development study found in 2003. The number of people working more than sixty hours a week has increased sharply in recent decades too. As a nation we have tended to follow American patterns of work, although not all Western countries have joined the flow. Western Europe (excluding the United Kingdom) has not generally followed suit. Europeans, according to the International Labor Organization, work 1,625 hours a year, compared with Americans who clock in 1,978 hours. In the US working hours have jumped dramatically in the last three decades with the average worker spending 199 more hours at work in 2000 than in 1973.[6]

Capitalism continues to require increased productivity and the ever-expanding working week delivers it, along with the spending power to sustain social status. As the working week extends for some, it has disappeared for many: the employed are working longer and longer days while the jobless numbers continue to increase. Genuine full-time jobs, as opposed to irregular part-time and casual jobs, have become a harder goal to achieve than ever for the disadvantaged.

The chest thumping about who was last out of the office and the legends built around the team that slept under the desk for several nights until a deal was clinched just keep coming. Full-time is taking on a whole new meaning these days. The trend to reward longer hours is reinforced by benefits and rewards. Employees are granted share options on the understanding they will work even harder to keep the stock price up in the future. The chargeable hours structure (where the hours spent on client work is recorded as billable hours, with certain targets to be met) in legal, professional services and other types of consulting also locks employees into increasingly onerous time demands. The ethos in many consulting firms informally rewards the employee with high chargeable hours, who becomes a hero and gains quick promotion, despite formal assurances that employees with lower 'client' hours are not penalised.

When a successful partner in a CBD law firm, busy with clients most of the time, moves to an equally senior but corporate role, such as staff partner, the transition is usually difficult. As one such partner told us, 'It meant I had to reassess what success was.' Suddenly the billable hours were not there as a sign of how much she contributed to the firm each day. And her status changed. The really powerful players in the professional services world are those with a top client list, and the 'rainmakers' who bring in more. The hours viewed as normal in servicing clients have expanded at the same time as technology has made everyone accessible. The notion that a lawyer or professional is unavailable is quaint – they are on call at any time, every day.

As the pressure builds to conform to greater time investment, the rhetoric on work/life balance grows ever louder, and the flow of information showing the effects of increased stress just keeps

coming. Along with the evidence of the inadequacy or unwilling-
ness of organisations to deal with the crisis, there's been increased
questioning of the over-arching long hours culture. Concerns
about how to raise children while both parents are in paid
employment have resulted in some tinkering with childcare places
and family leave provisions. In Australia in 2003, the Howard
Federal Government nominated family and work issues as a key
challenge. Anne Summers points out in her book *The End of
Equality* that women's pay and conditions have not just stalled
but have often deteriorated despite earlier signs of improvement.[7]
The failure is at a political level and across society. In the workplace even small gains have been eroded and the very subject of
women's rights virtually removed from the agenda. The notion of
power being equally shared between men and women at work is
laughable to many white-collar females. At a seminar hosted by
the Equal Opportunity in the Workplace Agency in Sydney in
2003, a group of professional women laugh bitterly when a male
executive says they should ideally be happy and optimistic as they
come to work every day. Over coffee, one of the audience
comments that the fight towards equality has only locked women
into a fruitless battle for a mythical even playing field. 'There's no
equality at home either, where I do all the work,' she adds.

The options are pretty bleak for women on the so-called
'mummy track' at work, but not many aspire to the male career
path either. Until recently, even token efforts to encourage women
in the workforce had little impact on the structure of jobs because
everyone was supposed to be striving for the same goal. Climb the
ladder or get out of the workforce, was the prevailing attitude.
Trading the original notion of women's liberation for the goal of
equality hasn't quite ended up the way many thought it would. At
least liberation theoretically includes discarding traditional gender
roles for new models, at home and at work. But long hours in both

paid and unpaid work is the crucial issue for many working mothers, not only a failure to get that promotion. Even well-educated, professional women find it hard to survive. For one of us the process of moving from full-time worker to mother and then back into the workplace was a draining and, at times, distressing process which was all about a struggle to keep afloat on two fronts: the domestic and the workplace.

Interestingly, the public debate may have fallen away but popular culture has caught up with this fraught issue. In her novel *I Don't Know How She Does It*, Allison Pearson creates a frighteningly familiar scenario of a working mother, bound to her job but perpetually in the grip of chronic guilt about the little time she spends with her two small children. From the smug nanny to the awful work colleagues and weary husband, Pearson's book has just about every element of working motherhood down pat. Reviewing the novel, author Katha Pollitt says the book is right about modern life being organised around the split between home and work: 'If it remains in place working mothers will always be holding down two full-time jobs, only one of which is paid and both of which are based on outmoded notions of gender roles'.[8]

Parents usually struggle with the dilemma of childcare and many patch together whatever system they can find and afford. Most of the care on offer does not acknowledge the reality of working life. Long day care, when it's available, may be designed around work hours, but once children are at school the equation gets much more difficult. To the dismay of many parents, the workplace and the school system continue to run in parallel lines, while organisations trot out rhetoric about family friendly policies that are more lip service than reality. There's no group more aware of this than working mothers. The issues surrounding kids and work appear depressingly circular and attempts to analyse and solve the problems seem to go nowhere.

Parents are not the only group struggling with these dilemmas, of course. Everyone has family, and many need time for a range of demands, such as providing care and company for an elderly parent. Then there are the singles who may be trying to have a life or find a partner, or simply pursue an interest.

Rather than looking to the organisation for any kind of help many employees are realising it is up to them to find their own way through to a more viable working pattern. The black and white assumptions by large organisations, politicians and institutions, that you get your satisfaction in life from either work or family and never the twain shall meet, is being challenged by people demanding a redesign of jobs.

There's a significant gap between the informal and formal organisational response to the dilemma – it's fine to have the family leave provisions but many workplaces can't cope when employees actually use that leave. The paternalism that characterised the organisations of the 1950s and 1960s has been ailing, but in the last few years it finally keeled right over. The workplace doesn't have the will or the wherewithal to consider employees' needs on an individual basis.

Mothers of young babies often laugh about the selective deafness that afflicts partners when the child cries at night. There's a corporate blindness, we believe, which appears to affect the senior management of many businesses. The head of an accounting firm told us he was genuinely perplexed by the flow of talented women out of his firm. They were going to other jobs, so he knew it wasn't a case of dropping right out of the workforce. He just couldn't work out why they left, he said. Yet the wonder is that any women, much less those with a family, stay in these environments, where long hours are the only passport to decent work and promotion, and the practices are primarily dictated by men, many of whom have wives who run their homes. This blindness by management extends to the demands of younger workers. An increasing number of employees from the next generation don't hesitate to move on if an employer doesn't provide suitable working conditions. The fluid nature of work and individual autonomy is challenging workplace structures.

Long hours are not a gender- or parent-specific problem. In fact, the impact is so widespread that it is becoming a mainstream rather than a gender issue. Far from easing work stress by spending longer on tasks, many people working long hours are actually putting more pressure on themselves, according to Australian research on the cult of long hours. Academics at Griffith University found that a large number of participants in a survey they conducted on hours at work were internalising the need to spend longer at the desk.[9] In fact, the researchers found, there are two key ways to get more hours from employees: one is for managers to coerce, but the other is to rely on the internalisation of pressure. When the standards for doing a good job become intrinsically linked with long hours and are reinforced in the workplace, there's no need to force employees. It appears to be just the way things are. Workers see the tangible rewards of long hours too – more money and a better lifestyle. Without a job there is no access to the trappings of success or status. And for many people, work has gradually become an easier realm to negotiate and gain satisfaction from – far cleaner than the messiness of relationships, intimacy and family.

Despite the demand for more hours on the job, the corporation has not only failed to come up with any answers to the ensuing problems, but it continues to offer a largely inflexible structure to negotiate within. Many more workers are realising this implacable reality, if not the economic and social reasons for the system's triumph. 'I am sick of managers reacting to every request for some flexibility as a problem,' a senior HR manager at a large financial organisation told us. 'If they just listened they would realise most people have figured out their own solution, at least partly, and it can usually work.' The women surveyed by Sylvia Ann Hewlett in *Baby Hunger* believed 'the long hours culture has become so oppressive that tinkering around at the margins no longer does the trick – at least not if you are interested in having a family'.[10]

In fact, according to sociologist Arlie Hochschild, many of us are in danger of applying the very principles of efficiency that underpin our jobs to our home lives. She has written extensively about the commercialisation of the intimate parts of life – how many executives farm out the care of their children to others, and even pay to have their chores done. Women have been co-opted to the work sphere without any fundamental change to the traditional domestic arrangements and this has led to many emotional as well as practical dilemmas. Women are the most recent recruits to the workforce, she writes, but the membership is offered in the 'same harsh terms as those offered' to men. 'The result makes for a harshness of life that seems so normal to us we don't see it.'[11] Nothing short of a revolution in our society and thinking so that care and the role of carers is rewarded as much as market success is needed, Hochschild concludes.

So the way many people work is changing the very way they live. The internalisation of work standards means every aspect of life becomes tied to the job. Our time has become commodified and divided into chunks to be allocated against key priorities. Family life may be held up as a linchpin of our society, but in reality, Hochschild says, that is not the case these days. 'Increasingly, our belief that family comes first conflicts with the emotional draw of both workplace and mall.'[12] She goes so far as to say the culture of capitalism is so powerful it actually swamps the family and community realms in importance, despite our emotional and even sentimental attachment to them. When relationships and family are organised around work, then child-bearing itself is often postponed until a career is established or it is sacrificed altogether.

When the worlds of work and family overlap, as working parents know only too well, the result is highly emotional. The distress of a parent unable to spend time with their children must be offered up to maintain a lifestyle, or they must seek an alternative. That's why some more pragmatic terms are being used to reflect the way some people are negotiating the long hours culture and weaving other strands into their lives. Research by the US Families and Work Institute coined the term 'dual-centric' to describe a group of senior executives who are able to successfully hold down a job and run a family and other commitments.[13] The group identified was a small slice of the respondents, but they were in senior positions in large organisations. The dual-centrics were surprisingly successful in their career progression (assessed by their seniority and salary), reported high levels of satisfaction in their lives *and* they worked fewer hours (around five hours less) each week than their colleagues. The researchers concluded the group did not look at their lives as a balancing act – trading off one set of values for another. People in this group simply worked out what they could do that worked for them and stuck to it. Many had children and were involved in the school system and in their communities, and made a point of not taking work home with them.

Not only senior managers are working out a new way of operating. Many younger workers are looking for new ways to reorganise their work and personal lives more satisfactorily. When he works within organisations, running seminars and workshops on balance and stress, academic Graeme Russell finds a discernible surge of interest in personal options about how to handle work/life issues. It's a noticeable change from when he started out thirty years ago studying and researching work/family balance, especially from the perspective of fathers, and workplace flexibility. Many workers are willing to invest their efforts in a job if it provides intellectual stimulation or a good income. But there are limits, Russell is finding, to this investment. Work is relied on to provide meaning but many employees are questioning the sacrifices and submersion of identity required.[14]

Now concerned executives are turning to him for advice about how to extract themselves from a long hours culture. They are also asking what is happening to the workplace, what the value of long hours really is to a business and whether it is delivering the output expected. While senior management appear to be holding the corporate line, that's often not the case informally. Something is happening with people at senior levels, according to Russell. Data is building to support this anecdotal evidence: fifty per cent of senior executives in a study Russell conducted said long hours and the balance issue does have a significant impact on their lives. The 2003 Mt Eliza Leadership Study, an annual survey of management published in the *Mt Eliza Business School Journal*, found balance was the top priority for the managers interviewed.[15] And there's a new word entering the rhetoric – people are talking about 'sustainability' of the long hours culture.

For those lucky enough to have interesting work (most of the time), there is a willing investment in hours if the need arises. Working hard on a major project provides intellectual stimulation as well as being career enhancing. Work can sometimes give a buzz and intellectual rewards that other parts of existence simply can't deliver. It therefore provides meaning and a focus that is hard to live without and it becomes addictive, sometimes even replacing fundamental aspects of life.

But even at the top there are boring and highly stressful elements of work that provide little reward. The difference between the long hours on the job for something rewarding and mere drudgery is evident. So too is the difference between doing the hard yards, as many small business owners do, when you have control over that investment and when you do not.

The recognition of the all-encompassing level of time commitment now required in the workplace is occurring in white-collar, professional circles as well as other sectors such as processing or manufacturing jobs. It is in these professional jobs that other symptoms of work dissatisfaction are also beginning to surface. The relationship between long hours and work is one element but the other is the failure to sustain relationships outside of the job. The time and energy – mental and physical – needed for partners, a sex life and family relationships simply disappear. The job sucks up the entire person. Our lust for the job erodes our lust for each other.

Graeme Russell observes: 'We know from data that people are sustained by close relationships and to progress in the workplace is related to the level of support we get. For a lot of people in those jobs the pressure is ongoing and there's an impact on their ability to regenerate outside.'[16] There is no energy left for personal life. And for some workers the job provides an easier place to establish relationships, making it more attractive than time-consuming socialising. Work begins to affect our ability to switch off – to clock out of work mode. It's a skill we are all losing as work becomes so pervasive. One manager told Russell of struggling to find the energy to switch on when he got home. He simply didn't have the capacity to do that.

The impact of addiction to the job is no longer confined to the work realm. Now it is having an impact on workers' capacity to be an effective person after work. Russell's study found that work pressures were having a discernibly negative effect on the relationships the employee has outside the workplace. The results revealed forty-five per cent of the 4,000 respondents, all working in a large

Australian organisation, believed 'work demands caused "generally poor quality relationships"'. When the study concentrated on managers the picture was worse. Half the male managers said work impacted on their time with their partner, but eighty per cent of their partners believed this was the case. Russell even suggested corporations should start running 'intimate relationship impact analysis' to understand the impact the long hours and pressure at work is having on relationships. Interestingly, men under thirty-five years were less willing to put up with the effects of long hours – sixty-three per cent of them said 'they would refuse a job or promotion if it had a negative impact on family life or their partners' careers'.[17] For single workers the demands of the job can even cancel out the prospect of a relationship or personal life.

When Juliet Schor wrote her seminal book on the subject of work hours, *The Overworked American*, in 1991, it was many years before the dot com boom helped fan the idea that you could spend all day and night at work and love it. Yet Schor's observations are eerily familiar. Instead of the changes she hoped would revitalise the social and business realms in the United States, it could be argued the world went the other way in the last decade, locking many of us into more time at the desk, not less. Flexible work policies, if they exist, are often not used because they still spell career death. And, as we have examined part-time work is no option at all for most professionals. For these people work increasingly replaces other sources of meaning and the addiction to work is becoming an addiction to long hours in the office. But there's a difference between working well and working longer; between commitment and not having enough time to see the kids or talk to your partner.

There is now pressure to work harder and to get satisfaction from the slog. This requires even more psychological investment, draining the worker of energy for relationships or, for many women, the time for marriage and children. Work has to take on more meaning or it fails us – and if our identity hinges on the job, that's a failure too hard to contemplate. When job cuts hit, for example, the impact is usually devastating for those being made redundant. Many feel a sense of personal failure and grief that goes beyond concern about finding another job and income. Work is so much a part of our identity that it's hard to know what to do without it and a growing number of redundant workers even require a version of grief counselling to help re-establish themselves professionally and in their private lives.

A decade ago, Schor concluded the answer to breaking the long hours cycle lay with intervention on a social level – from governments, unions, professional associations and other collective organisations.[18] With the benefit of hindsight it's clear that government intervention has generally been misguided or ineffective. In the UK, Prime Minister Tony Blair's work/life campaign has generated lots of hot air but little action. Launched in 2000, the program promised to tackle the long hours culture, target sectors with acute work/life balance problems and provide support and guidance.[19] Just a year after kicking off the brave new world of officially sanctioned work/life balance in the UK, a survey of HR professionals by the UK Chartered Institute of Personnel and Development found they generally believed that cutting back hours through part-time work, job sharing or compression of the working week was detrimental to career prospects.[20] Other critics pointed out the lack of clout the new program actually had to trigger real change, despite polls showing that flexibility was ranked in front of salary or benefits by job hunters.[21]

A more realistic approach to the realities of work as part of life underpins the way some European cultures handle organisational life. In the Netherlands there is autonomy to adjust working hours without a formal program to sanction the changes. The

Netherlands has addressed the issue of balancing work and parenting 'by providing all parents with greater control over their working hours' with a recently introduced law granting employees the right to request shorter or longer hours at work.[22] Employers must comply with the request unless there is a business reason to refuse. The aim is to allow parents to opt for part-time hours without concern about losing their jobs. Other countries in the European Union are considering introducing or have introduced flexible conditions. Sometimes this involves allowing parents to work fewer hours per week while their children are young and increasing hours later.

In Australia there are signs the whole raft of concerns around work, long hours and quality of life is becoming mainstream. In 2004, the recently appointed leader of the Australia Labor Party, Mark Latham, announced a shadow ministry to address work/life balance and stated his belief this was now a political issue.

Within many large organisations, however, well-meaning but often futile programs have led to little progress. Work/life balance programs are stymied unless bosses lead by example and most still don't. More than that, these programs are often seen as detrimental to the bottom line performance of a company. In late 2002 a group of HR executives in New York told *Workforce* magazine that, some flexibility aside, they were finding it difficult to create a 'culture that supports these programs.'[23] In fact, the article concluded that data from the US Bureau of Labor Statistics suggests virtually no growth in work/life programs in recent years. And the link between long hours and career advancement was retaining a firm grip on employees. People are actually penalised for trying to achieve better work/life balance, according to psychoanalyst and men's health therapist Stephen Carroll, who hears of executives being hauled over the coals at performance review time for taking off a morning or two to attend a school concert.[24] The resistance to the idea of flexibility and shorter hours is systemic and reinforced continuously by senior managers who simply don't believe in the idea, who have got where they are because they are good at dealing with stress, or feel obliged to keep up the bottom line rhetoric.

The nature of the business world means any downtime is now considered fair game by the system. Perhaps that's not so surprising. The much vaunted time-saving from new technology never made work hours shorter because market forces found plenty of productivity to be wrung from the time liberated by computers. It seems almost naïve now to think that could have been the assumption. On paper, of course, it seems like a perfectly rational proposition. Save time here and shorten the turnaround on producing a report or service there, and surely the number of units produced can rise proportionately. But this type of thinking relies on a robotic view of human effort and rather conveniently ignores some critical elements of how we think and use knowledge. In service firms, the numbers and demands of clients simply ratchet up to meet the new, more efficient time cycle that comes from better processes and technology.

With this increase and emphasis on productivity, there must be a limit to how far people can be pushed to keep up with technology. 'There has to be a release valve somewhere,' says Leigh Clapham, 'but it may require a reassessment of what top job performance means and the psychology that management uses to reinforce the effort.

'I think human nature has a threshold. I can't say we've reached the threshold but as it gets tighter and tighter there will be a slowing down of expectations. Maybe it will manifest in being a little more generous in our praise of people's achievements. I know from my own observations the manner in which you praise someone in a job is important. You can give them too much confidence so they slow down. But they need encouragement.'

The progress in reshaping work beyond some superficial measures often comes from individuals opting out or recalibrating the work schedule. Sometimes, the redesign of a career can mean deliberately opting for more repetitive but less stressful occupations. Stephen Carroll sees quite a few lawyers from firms where the longer the hours worked, the more heroic they are considered. It's a badge of honour to work till midnight for weeks on end for some of them, but those who seek Carroll's advice are very aware of the need to change. Often they switch jobs, like the thirty-something lawyer who decided to swap his high-level work at a law firm to become a conveyancer. Although he finds the work less interesting, he now has time with his family. Carroll also has a number of clients who are multi-part-timers with up to five different jobs.

As journalists, we've seen first-hand how part-time jobs can work. For some employees, flexible hours that allow them to spend more time with their family are a reality. Sometimes the changes employees make to redress the work/life balance are less dramatic and on a much smaller scale. Leigh Clapham makes it a rule to get home for dinner unless he is travelling. Often people simply have to learn to clock off again. The official acknowledgement of the repercussions of excessive work hours is some way off, but it's bubbling below the surface. If, as Juliet Schor points out, the work ethic itself is, in some sense, a time ethic, a re-examination of the hours needed to do a job effectively is well overdue. Employees are not passive in the face of these pressures: they are taking the issue into their own hands, where they can.

The dismantling of the long hours culture can be viewed differently if jobs and careers are re-examined. Redesigning jobs is a skill in demand these days. Graeme Russell uses a hypothetical exercise in his work with organisations. He tells seminar groups they have to reorganise their work into three days a week and they are then asked to redesign their job. He has found eighty-five per cent of people can redesign their jobs, but they see it as a huge barrier to look at things differently. And career redesign, although viable for some, presents an even greater hurdle.

At Vodafone Australia, manager of brand and people Deb Howcroft tells of the countless discussions she conducts with people wanting a new way of working. 'The number of people I have interviewed who say "I left my previous job because I couldn't get work/life balance and I want that in my life" is amazing. They want a commitment on that. They want to know it's acceptable to work when they want. They are demanding it and they are making decisions about their careers based on it. Good people, senior people, will opt out it they are not supported with this stuff.'[25]

Vodafone is not the only company doing this and Howcroft says it is received well because the employees need to feel they are being supported as whole people, no matter what the commercial reality. The friction between corporate lip service and reality is growing increasingly discernible to workers of all ages: Baby Boomers may be held responsible for establishing workaholic habits but the next generation entering the workforce is unlikely to want to live that way.

Despite the bleak picture our research conveys, most of the professionals and academics we spoke to believe the employees will eventually win the battles and then the war. Jill Andresky Fraser reached the same conclusion in her book *White Collar Sweatshop*. While the data she cites is gloomy, tracing the increasing hours, relatively lower pay, holidays and benefits of US office workers over the last decade, she nevertheless ends on a positive note. Workers voting with their feet and their wallets are attacking the sweatshop organisation, she argues.[26]

The fluidity of jobs can make it easier to do just that. A TV advertisement for the Fairfax-owned online recruitment service, mycareer.com, shows a smug boss walking out of his office and noting his employees are working through their lunchbreak. It's clear he is a slave-driver and his staff are fed up. And it becomes apparent to viewers that several employees are already looking for other jobs on the Internet while the boss stands gloating over their enslavement.

This increasing mobility will be aided by further stripping away the myth of the paternal organisation. When loyalty is no longer rewarded with security of employment, employees will continue to withdraw their commitment. The failure of flexibility and balance programs in the corporate sphere trigger questioning of organisational values and practices.

Most employees no longer expect the corporate to take a paternal role or even provide the answers to work/life dilemmas. But they do expect the right and the mental and physical space to run their personal lives.

The struggle to work and raise children or have a personal life are very real concerns for many people. In today's workplaces there's an often implicit requirement of full commitment in return for a job, leaving little time or energy for anything else. It's a transaction that simply didn't operate in such black and white terms even a decade or so ago.

---

1. Janet Perna addressed the 'Diversity in Leadership' lunch, hosted by the NSW Department of Women on 8 May 2003.
2. '2003 World Population Data Sheet', Population Reference Bureau, July 2003.
3. Reported in Henley, Jon. 'A mixed blessing', *The Guardian*, 10 October 2003.
4. Schor, Juliet. op cit., p. 4.
5. 'Social trends 2003', The Australian Bureau of Statistics.
6. 'Key indicators of the labour market 2001–2002', International Labor Organisation.

7. Summers, Anne. *The End of Equality*. Random House Australia, 2003.
8. Pollitt, Katha 'In the family's way', *London Review of Books*, 9 September 2003.
9. Griffith Work Time Project. 'Working time transformations and effects', Griffith University, April 2003.
10. Hewlett, Sylvia Ann. *Baby Hunger: The New Battle for Motherhood*. Atlantic Books, 2002, p. 233.
11. Hochschild, Arlie. *The Commercialization of Intimate Life*. University of California Press, 2003, p. 8.
12. Ibid. p.143.
13. Galinsky, Ellen. *Dual-Centric: A New Concept of Work-Life*. US Families and Work Institute, 2003.
14. Interview with Graeme Russell.
15. Fox, Catherine. 'Leaders working for a balanced life', *The Australian Financial Review*, 11 February 2003, p. 58.
16. Interview with Graeme Russell.
17. Reported in Horin, Adele. 'Boss wants to hear about your sex life', *The Sydney Morning Herald*, 8 September 2003, p. 3.
18. Schor, op cit., p. 136.
19. 'Work/Life Balance Campaign media release', UK Department of Trade and Industry, 9 March 2000.
20. Reported in Abrahams, Geraldine. 'Humans as Resources?', *The Glasgow Herald*, 26 June 2003.
21. Reported in Ward, Lucy. 'Workers put a premium on flexible hours', *The Guardian*, 2 January 2003.
22. OECD. 'Babies and bosses – reconciling work and family life', Vol 1, (Australia, Denmark and the Netherlands), Paris, 2002.
23. Hansen, Fay. 'Truths and myths of work/life balance', *Workforce*, December 2002.
24. Interview with Stephen Carroll.
25. Interview with Deb Howcroft.
26. Andresky Fraser, op cit., p. 229.

9

Creatives v. careerists: the clash of ideologies

Dexter Dunphy gets lots of calls from troubled and unhappy twenty-somethings.1 Given his teaching background at the Australian Graduate School of Management and the University of Technology in Sydney, the veteran academic and author has had more contact with young ambitious business students than most. But the calls are not about a failure to climb the corporate ladder or how to get that next promotion. Virtually all the callers are doing pretty well in their careers, often in investment banks, law firms, consulting or in the upper ranks of companies. What Dunphy is finding is that these otherwise textbook examples of careerists are hating their lives. They are profoundly disillusioned and can't really work out why everything they were striving for is such a letdown, or how they can make a change.

As a kind of mentor figure to these people, Dunphy tries to offer some advice or just a sympathetic ear. Mostly they want to talk about the crunch that comes a few years into a high pressure job, complete with long hours and heavy responsibility. They usually have the question: 'Why am I doing this?'.

'I talked to someone recently who heard me talking on the ABC and is in financial services. She's 27 and has done very well but found herself surrounded by people who didn't share her values. Her own attitudes were around spiritual and personal development,' Dunphy says. They had a long chat. The young woman was seriously thinking about leaving the job and finding something else. She wasn't about to opt out of a career altogether, because of financial commitments, but she was finding it genuinely difficult to continue in her work role.

Career dissatisfaction is not new and neither is an overwhelming feeling of pointlessness in a job that was meant to deliver. This is happening more often, and for a much younger group, than Dunphy has observed before. These people are not a bunch of bleeding hearts or seekers of enlightenment. They are well-educated and capable middle-class graduates who populate the professional services firms and the management ranks throughout corporate Australia and many Western countries. Their angst has also been noted by Charles Handy, who frequently finds himself fielding similar calls in the United Kingdom. The legacy of all that flurry around the new economy is playing itself out in the first decade of the new century, but in a mostly unexpected way.

If the experiences of Dunphy and Handy, both of whom have spent decades observing and writing about the business world, is anything to go by, there is more dissatisfaction than ever before. It's tempting to dismiss the concerns as a luxury for a bunch of well-off, even spoilt, members of society. After all, these are the people with access to good education and decent jobs. But that's part of the point – commentators are asking if this group is not committed to the project what does that say about our working lives? And these people are also the ones keen to use their lives productively for the organisation and society. Why can't a sophisticated business environment attempt to meet their needs and harness their energy?

Because of the common thread running through their concerns, social researchers are starting to identify this group as part of a larger, values-based and demographically disparate group in society. They have been labelled the 'cultural creatives' and are emerging as a potent force for change in society and business.

In the 1990s two American academics, Paul Ray and Sherry Ruth Anderson, were among the first to identify the common concerns binding these people and came up with the 'cultural creative' tag.[2] Ray runs a market research firm that specialises in polls on the lifestyle and values of Americans, while his wife, Anderson, is a psychologist. Years of market research into the role of values in the US way of life and research work with environmental groups began to show them a change was afoot. The description 'cultural creative' really describes a way of thinking shared by the group which is based on their desire for change, concern for the environment and the sustainability agenda, and their objections to many of the by-products of a multinational, globalised world. They are the group responsible for the interest in 'personal authenticity', or the alignment between actions and beliefs, and can range from the greenie who objects to the lack of recycling in their workplace to the feminist who organises a women's group in a company.

The research by Ray and Anderson was not focused on employees or the workplace. And it was carried out well before the dot com crash and the collapse of Enron, WorldCom and Australia's One.Tel and HIH. Even so, the studies picked up on some themes that became far more mainstream once these disasters unfolded – disenchantment and questioning of the market system and a challenging of corporate standards.

As a group, cultural creatives reject materialism as a central part of life, along with greed, displays of status, discrimination and social inequality, and they lack faith in many social institutions, from multinationals to government. But they are no less reliant on work than their colleagues. Our research and anecdotal evidence from years of writing about the Australian workforce suggests cultural creatives in the workforce here are not anti-business. They care more than most employees about the way business operates and want the workplace to be different – less hierarchical, less ruthless and less punishing to parents. They are just as involved in life outside the organisation as they are in the job. This may include involvement in the community, personal interests, study or family. Allocating time for these parts of life is so important to these types of people that they are reorganising their jobs to make room for these personal elements, and not the other way around.

Many years ago, during the booming 1980s, one of us interviewed the head of one of Australia's biggest investment banks. A highly successful executive, he had spent years pursuing his career, immersed in and driven by the financial markets. At a time when he had achieved everything he could wish for, and more, he was perplexed. Without actually saying so, he was wondering if there was anything more to life. His questioning went further than his own circumstances. Worried by the way behaviour in organisations could be so ruthless and amoral, he spoke about finding the balance between work and other parts of life in order to maintain perspective and ethics. The culture of the bank which he had helped to forge was not what he had envisaged. The people there, he said, often behaved in a way they never would at home.

In his quest for a more satisfying way of work he was turning to literature – a world he had never wanted to pursue, having left school quite early to get a job. As we talked about Virginia Woolf and his other newly discovered favourite authors it seemed like he had undergone some kind of metamorphosis. The interview was memorable although it would be easy to criticise his concerns as a timely indulgence once his fortune had been made. A few months after the September 11 disaster we spoke again briefly about the outlook for the business world. 'Business still doesn't get it,' he told us. His views were and are unusual. Many of his peers would never feel this way, even when they had left the corporate world behind.

The cultural creatives may not know it, but they are increasingly identified by researchers as part of a slow polarisation within organisations that has bypassed the change experts and management consultants so eager to be seen as the architects of corporate transformation. When we first started hearing about cultural creatives our reaction was sceptical. There have been many terms used over the years to describe sub-groups of the population, from their demographics (where they live and what they earn) to their psychographics (their values, beliefs and attitudes). During the 1980s there was talk of Yuppies and then we heard about DINKS (Double Income No Kids) and even more acronyms started appearing. Although they make a good headline, the use of such groupings can be limited. How accurate is a generalisation of how people think? Most of the time, this work is done by market researchers keen to more accurately profile consumer groups so marketers can effectively target them.

When the term 'cultural creatives' continued to occur in conversations with researchers, authors and academics, we decided it was worth a closer look. The way cultural creatives think and the issues that are important to them define this group of people. But the studies on which Ray and Anderson based their work were not driven by demand for a new consumer target. They were driven by a wish to connect the themes recurring in studies about values and work out how that translates to the way people live. This is not a sociological approach that ignores the work realm, as is often the case, or quarantines the social issues from those of the workplace. It acknowledges the meshing of these issues and the understanding of the power corporations hold in the community. The role of business and our relationship with work is a core concern for cultural creatives because that's where many of them spend a substantial part of their life. This is why, we believe, so many business thinkers have found the approach useful.

Our own interviews with executives and white-collar workers reinforced the sense that this is a framework with something valid to offer. Take the business executive we spoke to about work and career. Scott Walters was proud of his work achievements and was running an online broking business. As we sat in his glass-walled office the noises and activities of a busy workplace were easy to observe. The casually dressed staff, mainly in their late twenties, included a mix of men and women from various ethnic backgrounds. Usually the door to his office was open, he explained, as we discussed his attitude to the workplace and his job and how that had transformed over recent years.

His focus has changed dramatically, Walters told us, after spending twenty years in financial services and fifteen years as a stockbroker. It had always been important to him to get up in the morning feeling there was something to look forward to, and his choice of career was something he did not regret. But in other areas of his life he was taking stock.

'I love the market, the stories and variety – that keeps me interested. I like the opportunity to create and build and achieve success. I am motivated by success. I am in some respects egotistical: I like people to think I have done a good job even though I would need to acknowledge that it's the team behind me that has done that. That is still important to me, but at age forty-two I am also recognising that within me, I desire to give back.

'What I enjoyed ten years ago about work is different to what

I enjoy now. I do want to get more involved with community and the arts. So many people in positions of influence, when they retire, say they want to get on a board or work for a not-for-profit organisation: all very altruistic, but they are not in positions of power. That's why I am trying to do it now, because in this position I am more able to divert resources.'

Walters talked about his efforts to slowly change work practices, getting more women involved in decision making and into senior roles, dismantling layers of hierarchy and encouraging collaboration in a traditionally ruthless business. It was clear he invested quite a lot of his time in thinking about these issues. His management style was deliberately low key and he used a 'servant leadership' model – where the boss is there to provide advice and counsel rather than dictate the next move – for guidance. 'I'm here to act as a helper for others,' he explained, 'as well as steer the ship.'

Perhaps, he observed, the shorter and shorter tenure of CEOs is a symptom of them holding on to too much power and kudos, and becoming stale. They should be letting people below them shine and eventually take over the job rather than hanging on too long.

'I think the formality of the workplace has changed to be more informal. I think respect has declined in general in the workplace, opportunity has increased, and mobility. I think that change in formality means it's acceptable to go and have a coffee, you don't keep tabs on people, you don't bundy on or off: that's a big change. Work hours have increased, not decreased; even though contracts are still being written saying you will work thirty-seven hours a week. But I think people don't stick to set hours if they have something to complete. Lunch hours cut both ways; there's no such thing as someone who takes a set hour for lunch but it's also OK to take more than a set hour for lunch. Does the worker sort that out? It would be unstated or informally approved.'

He was struggling to change the embedded ethos of a highly

competitive industry, while giving autonomy and freedom to his staff. At the same time, his other life, the time with family and riding his beloved Harley Davidson, was of enormous importance to him. He was also keen to contribute to society and had a number of social responsibility goals for the firm, with several programs already running. Again, this was a part of his life to which he devoted much effort and planning.

'We've set up a community relations committee in the office – we now have thirteen people working several mornings a week with the Red Cross. I do that on Friday mornings and go out to talk to kids of drug addicts, neglected or with single parents. These are kids who would arrive with no breakfast at school and they are at a school for kids with behavioural problems. The volunteers go in and give them breakfast and we present a role model.

'This month is social relations month and we are divided into teams, raising money. People have brought in their videos from home and are renting them out to other staff and all the funds go to United Way [a non-profit, non-sectarian organisation that raises funds for local communities], and we have instituted a payroll deduction program with them. United Way targets eighty-three charities which may not get as much attention. I think we have 83 staff and 29 donating about $1,000 a month to United Way. This environment has provided me with the autonomy to do those kinds of things . . . allowing me to exercise my creative ability.'

At the same time his day is divided up with the aim of sharing time with family and community interests as well as work.

'There's no day that is the same as any other. The splits in time are all different. I like to spend forty to sixty per cent of my time on what I call strategic matters. I spend ten per cent on adminis-tration, signing letters and so on. I like to spend about another twenty to thirty per cent with the staff, either in meetings or walking the floor or having coffee with someone. Then the rest of my day is time I put into not-for-profit and the community. I'd like to think I could get to a situation in life where my life is a third, a third, a third: a third family, a third work and a third community.'

For Walters the new contract with work is about a reassessment of the role business has in society. 'There are people around town who don't think that's valid. That really work is work, or as Adam Smith said, "the business of business is business". The implication being that it is not the business of businesses to get involved in the community or philanthropy or anything like that. It is to deliver return to shareholders, increasing shareholder wealth. I guess I ask the question, how much is enough? When companies report $2 billion in profit, to me that's almost obscene. OK, I come from a bourgeois capitalist background and I work in a bourgeois industry and benefit from the trappings of that, but I think about where those funds could be better diverted. Not to the detriment of shareholders by any means, but the betterment of society. But that kind of concept of profit needs redefining.'[3]

By early 2004 Walters had redefined his own career as he prepared to move to a new job.

While the cultural creatives we have identified are at odds with many of their colleagues, they are not about to walk away. They want the workplace to change and they are as financially bound to work as most. But they can gradually start to use the leverage they sense is theirs to chip away at how the system works. They can replace standards of behaviour and productivity by gradually forging new ways of doing the job. Orders delivered from on high – the old command-and-control style – just don't work now. The notion that an organisation only exists for the bottom line is outdated and counterproductive for these people. What they want is not just the flexibility to attend a school concert or have a coffee break when they like. They need to see their work as useful and interesting and to question process and procedure. They don't look to the organisation for answers or even much support. They may turn down a promotion because they simply don't need the aggravation. They work hard if they are intellectually engaged but withdraw if they are not.

The tension in the workplace between cultural creatives and others is more discernible now because control, and how the organisation can impose it to keep productivity high, has moved further up the agenda for a broader group of employees. Better access to education and more information means some workers now know they have leverage through how much effort they put into a job. Cultural creatives typically want to align their personal values with their work. This doesn't mean shunning hard work but it does mean making work more fulfilling and being involved in work practices that go their way rather than the employer's way. These people are as hooked on work as anyone, but they refuse to offer themselves body and soul to the corporation. They are leading a backlash against the way the organisation has colonised and co-opted employees.

The polarisation between cultural creatives and others can generate change from within the ranks of companies. Cultural creatives tend to resist working for goals they don't believe in. They do not buy into prescriptive projects or team building and are dismissive of mission statements and corporate vision. Work carries much importance for them and organisations are recognised as an enormously powerful part of society. But they care just as much about changing workplace practices and questioning the role of business as they do about the next step up the corporate ladder. And when they feel strongly enough they speak up or try to make changes.

Cultural creatives stand at one end of the office spectrum while their opposites, the careerists or the money obsessed, stand at the other. Between these extremes, of course, lie many degrees of difference. Many people feel a duty to perform well but have not the same level of psychological commitment to the workplace, nor to society. Some may feel a real sense of insecurity about their jobs. They do not have high expectations about what work can deliver. Their level of curiosity about the psychology of work is likely to be lower too. We're not suggesting there is a wasteland between the driven ambitious workers and the creatives – after all, the workplace needs to include a range of people to do the work. One of the traps we see much management literature falling into is the assumption that everyone is burning to become CEO or go as far up the ladder as possible.

In a *Harvard Business Review* article on the importance of these kinds of people, the writers pointed out that in the United States a 'fierce work ethic has imposed a certain rigidity on assumptions about what motivates people on the job'.[4] Misconceptions about why we work abound. Not all employees are striving for the same goal, they do not want the same out of work, nor do they all want a promotion. And it is a big mistake to assume everyone wants to be a manager.

What makes cultural creatives unusual and noteworthy, in our opinion, is their obsession with changing the rules and offering a counterpoint to the career junkies who need a promotion like a hit. Sometimes cultural creatives get so fed up with the strictures of the organisation they trade it for free agency, even though it means more work. A talented colleague, in demand for his knowledge and flair, decided to leave staff writing roles for a freelance existence, even though he admits it takes him every hour of the day and far into the night to produce enough work to earn a decent income. But the thought of returning to a job within a company remains unappealing. He has freedom and feels he does a far better job being uncoupled from a corporate framework with which he often felt at loggerheads.

The move to more fluid workplaces, propped up by mobility through new technology, has contributed to this quiet revolution over the past decade. There's been a slow decrease in formality and respect in the workplace. Those with the ability to challenge work practices are increasingly doing so. We've talked in an earlier chapter about the notion of 'presenteeism', the idea that workers can be present at work but putting in minimal effort unless they are properly engaged by their job. In these ways even those workers undertaking process tasks may force some change in their day-to-day activities. Others may choose a less negative route. When the NAB began running workshops to ask for process improvement ideas the management team was surprised by the number of suggestions that emerged from staff who wanted to do things differently and more efficiently. If these efforts continue they can add up to a loosening of control of management and cultural creatives are well aware of this.

The defining of cultural creatives has been picked up by other writers and researchers. In his book *The Rise of the Creative Class* Richard Florida says cultural creatives tend to be clustered in certain occupations, such as science, architecture, design, writing and the arts as well as those in jobs in the business world and other sectors where creativity makes up the main part of their work.[5]

This creative class is becoming a force to be reckoned with because of their intellectual property and the value that this contributes to the bottom line in many commercial enterprises, adding up to more leverage to negotiate the kind of workplace that suits them. Nobody likes to be constantly micro-managed but creative people tend to dislike it more than most. In fact, it restricts them from using their creativity. Managers using traditional methods of supervision and control with creatives are finding more and more that it slows productivity, and are being forced to find different ways of dealing with these types of employees.

'Whereas the lifestyle of the previous organisational age emphasised conformity, the new lifestyle favours individuality, self-statement, acceptance of difference and the desire for rich, multi-dimensional experiences,' Florida writes.[6]

For Scott Walters, one of the overwhelmingly positive aspects of the way the workplace is beginning to operate is the freedom to be creative as a result of the blurring of the lines between work and the rest of life. 'What it allows in people is creativity. If you could be critical of the old days, and the workforce then, you couldn't be creative. You couldn't, if you had an idea at 5 p.m., stay and work on it: you were out the door and the idea was lost. You are now free to exercise your own creative talents subject to your performing.' This is the upside to the blurring of personal and professional life – the boundaries don't matter and sometimes that makes work far more satisfying. There is time for creativity to blossom.

The role of the organisation (as we have contended) remains a strong one: organisations still matter a lot and they are not going away. Just as cultural creatives are working from within to bring about organisational change, Florida says the creative class is nurtured by small and large companies which can provide the environment for creativity to flourish. The reason the creative class has arisen has a lot to do with intellectual value being more important than ever. The issue of who controls creativity is not about employer versus employee or intellectual property rights, it is 'how to keep tapping the creative furnace inside each human being.'[7]

Dexter Dunphy believes that there is a struggle going on between traditional business methods (the 'business as usual' mindset) and those who believe business should not and cannot survive as it is. It reflects a growing consciousness of the power employees have in a knowledge economy, where they can choose what level of commitment to the job they will bring to work, where technology lets them compare their workplace with many others and they feel confident to voice their discontent.

The clash between mindsets takes many forms. In some companies we have even seen the CEO attempting to change the business, only to find resistance from management and the board. Executive after executive we have spoken to over the last few years tell us similar stories about a desire to change their culture and improve the workplace. But it is a much harder task than they anticipate, and they usually meet implacable opposition from the supporters of the status quo. Former CEO of investment bank ABN AMRO Australia, Steve Crane, says he worries about some changes being made in the way employees treat each other because it might earn them the reputation of being 'too nice'[8] to clinch a deal. Managers are threatened by change just as many workers are. Democracy in the workplace is actually resisted by many employees, as Brazilian businessman Ricardo Semler discovered. 'Workers are so conditioned by society to accept a paternalistic hierarchy that at first glance, democracy looks like chaos.'[9]

The disillusionment many people feel about the way business operates has only increased with the wave of corporate collapses in recent years. Even those employees more interested in money and career are experiencing doubts about the system, Dunphy believes, as they watch the fallout from the greed and duplicity that these major company collapses reveal. It's a level of doubt stemming from a growing lack of trust in the corporate sphere, where even careerists are likely to take a second look at the gap between rhetoric and reality.

What is the solution? Another generation of culture change programs is not the answer. That's exactly the kind of sham humanism that rubs cultural creatives up the wrong way. Being forcefed a package of values in order to find commitment to their job is the antithesis of what cultural creatives desire. No search for purpose delivered by the organisation as a neat package will make much impact on a group like the cultural creatives. Many of these elaborate efforts at cultural change tend to fail at a practical level, even if their intentions sound noble. In fact, cultural creatives are looking for a renewed sense of community which has little in common with the individualism of American-style capitalism, which also pervades the Australian business world.

Understanding cultural creatives and the creative class will trigger change in organisations. Cultural creatives are interested in (even driven by) the need to redefine work and job expectations. They seek some sense of purpose from work but often do not find it. They want work to have significance but it must be framed by different values which reflect their belief in sustainability, fairness and diversity. Many of them are obsessed with work, not just because they seek meaning through it, but also because they want to make a difference to how business operates and its role in society. There is a new wave of 'meaning seeking', where many people are asking, 'If it's only about making money why is it dominating my whole life?'

As a result, they are not interested in being 'free agents', but equally they don't want to be controlled. Nor do they want to be told what it is to be 'authentic' by a team of management consultants. They will find a voice as traditional hierarchies crumble and knowledge becomes the predominant currency in organisations. This is not a club with membership or exclusivity of rights. It's a style and way of engaging your mind with the workplace in a different way. And it's about identity.

---

1. Interview with Dexter Dunphy.
2. Ray, Paul and Anderson, Sherry. *The Cultural Creatives*. Three Rivers Press, 2000.
3. Interview with Scott Walters.
4. DeLong, Thomas J., and Vijayaraghavan, Vineeta. 'Let's hear it for the B team', *Harvard Business Review*, June 2003.

5. Florida, Richard. *The Rise of the Creative Class*. Perseus Books, 2002, p. 13.
6. Ibid. p. 29.
7. Ibid. p. 15.
8. Fox, Catherine. 'The people dividend', *AFR BOSS*, November 2002.
9. Semler, Ricardo. *The Seven-Day Weekend*. Random House, 2003, p. 144.

10

Personality plus: getting it right at work

A T THE ELITE CHICAGO RESTAURANT Charlie Trotter's, the story goes, waiters are so dedicated to diners that they wear double-sided adhesive tape on the soles of their shoes to collect any wandering lint that might spoil the atmosphere.

When we read this in a copy of the left-wing journal, *The Baffler*, edited by author and historian Tom Frank, the message we're meant to receive is negative.[1] Here's an employer who will go to bizarre lengths to provide the perfect dining experience. The identity of the individual merges with the work: at Charlie Trotter's waiters must take on the boss's project from head to toe.

As fans of Frank and *The Baffler*, we can see what the magazine is getting at but wonder whether this is really so bad. Do the waiters truly lose their identity by picking up the lint? Are they automatons when their bodies turn into cleaning machines? We don't think so. It's pretentious and silly to worry about the crumbs quite so slavishly but we figure the workers are still able to protect their individual selves.

The question of how far people should go to accommodate the workplace is an important one at a time when companies seek alignment between the organisation and its employees. Boards and CEOs are urged to understand and then corral their workers if they want to be competitive. It's a dual approach. On one hand, companies must appreciate what drives people if they want to attract the most talented, especially in the knowledge economy where power means ideas and brains, not just strength. On the other hand, you need your employees to be on side, sharing the attitudes, behaviour and personality of the company. Moulding employees' values is now an overt mission of big corporations. They make no secret of their desire to match employee desires with those of the company and many of them spend a lot of money on programs to model and shape common attitudes.

Some companies, like banks, where service and handling of customers is important in retaining market share, have been particularly active in programs to change internal cultures and style. Asking the staff to be nice to customers isn't quite enough any more: apart from anything else, banks spent the best part of the 1990s forcing staff to work faster and do more, something unlikely to leave much time or energy to be pleasant at the front counter. If anything, the banks are now being forced to clean up their own mess after years when relationships with staff were damaged. Now they have started workplace discussions around the values of the business and how it should be run.

Many other employees have been affected by this move from the bosses to get them onside. Even if you don't have a formal culture change program underway in your organisation, it's likely that your managers have been influenced by a body of literature, theory and practice directed at changing the mindset of the worker. It's easy to be cynical about some of these programs and to question just how open an organisation or a leadership team is to values that challenge the culture too deeply. Many of the programs are new and it will be years before companies can really judge how much impact they have. But the push to create perfect workers is on.

Social and community attitudes are in constant flux and this is an age of tremendous scientific and technological change. Human beings can now control their bodies and lives in ways they once did not think possible. A whole raft of things – from the shape of your nose to whether you can procreate – is no longer a matter of nature but up to you to decide. We remake and reinvent our personalities and our dreams. It would be amazing if organisations did not believe they could intervene in the way people think and behave at work.

That's the rational explanation. The reality is that the pressure on employees to be a certain way at work and to manipulate their personalities and behaviour to suit the boss can be irritating or even frightening to many people. In the twenty-first century, Western workers are less likely to be physically exploited, given that so much work is now 'weightless'. But some feel emotionally exploited by the requirement to package themselves in an accept-able fashion for work.

Even the junior knows that part of the deal at work is to laugh at the boss's jokes and be very careful about challenging his or her views. When the compliance is so overt, it's easy enough for employees to separate it from their authentic selves. They know when they are kowtowing to the boss and can mark it up as expe-rience. You acquiesce in order to achieve. In fact, the denial of your own views, in certain situations, is seen as sensible, mature behaviour, essential for survival in a workplace. Younger workers, in particular, may operate seamlessly at two levels – they are far from overawed by senior managers but they have figured out the practical requirement to comply with the dominant culture of the office.

But the further we go up the chain, the longer we spend at work, the older we get and the more we have invested in survival, the more likely we are to feel the weight of expectation around how we behave. This is when employees can feel that their identities are under siege and become more aware of the disconnection between what they think outside and inside the workplace.

As many of us are overtaken by work, it can sometimes seem that our personalities are being overtaken by the way we operate at the office. Even if you like your job, most of us grapple some of the time with the balance between what you think of as your *real* identity and the second self you bring to the office. For many people, the pressure to merge public and private selves and behaviour is a critical test of their ability to negotiate their way through the politics and culture of the office. As work begins to take up more emotional space, there is less chance to retain a separate 'you' and more pressure to develop a persona that suits the workplace.

Cultural theorist Meaghan Morris says we develop a 'viable personality' in order to survive at work. We may never articulate the way we operate in the office yet know instinctively that there are rules to be followed and that we must operate in a certain way. Morris puts it this way: 'You can't be needy, you can't be a drama queen – except in some specific areas where that is rewarded. You can't be boring, or flaccid, you can't be down, you can't be dull. You have to be cool, but warm.'[2] A British man employed in advertising says: 'You almost have to have a second persona. You have to be non-emotional and strictly professional. People talk about being one big happy family but the reality is different.'[3]

Corporate cool mixed with flight-deck warmth seems to be the essential style in many companies, especially for women, among whom there's an emerging homogeneity. There's less requirement of men to be warm and more pressure on them to be in command and in control, while at the same time being open and chummy. For everyone, there's a suite of characteristics to follow.

In the past, workers simply had to cooperate and 'cop it sweet' to survive, says Morris. In many ways your personality was suspended at work or at least it was not a crucial element of whether or not you would succeed. But in a knowledge economy where the product is often based on ideas, personality plays a bigger role. Often workers have no specific skills other than their ability to articulate an idea, present a report, outline a vision. That's where personality makes a difference. At almost every management forum now, the emphasis is on the value of people and their creativity. Even organisations which, in reality, need people to perform relatively routine tasks as efficiently as possible will talk about the importance of employees' ideas.

The focus on identity is increasing, according to academic Carl Rhodes. 'You see it when you look at the Saturday recruitment ads in the paper,' he says. 'Most of the stuff is about the sort of person you are. They ask for team players, they ask about communication skills, about your motivation. This is all about identity.'[4]

The increased focus on behaviour and personality rather than skills is evident in the growth of services like coaching. Coaches are increasingly called in by companies to help change the style of workers, especially managers. Harry Onsman, a Melbourne-based management consultant, says this is part of the shift from a manager who directs his employees to one who acts more as a facilitator for staff: 'Of course organisations still want managers who are technically competent in their jobs but they also want managers who can bring out the best in other people.'[5]

There's often a rather dumbed-down approach to the type of person who will bring out the best in others. Management gurus produce manuals and lists of the kind of nurturing, inclusive behaviour expected from a boss, often with little appreciation of the vagaries of human nature. One of us once worked with a boss who was grumpy, demanding and not especially gregarious or good with people. Yet his high standards and the fact that he cared passionately about his craft meant that his team lifted, stuck together and worked well. He would have failed any nurturing test but his style was effective. It's worth remembering those maverick operators, the outriders, at a time when corporate behaviour is very prescribed and when workers are asked to limit any emotional noise that might interfere with productivity.

Amanda Sinclair, a management professor at the Melbourne Business School, says the persona required by today's organisation tends to be 'pretty unreflective, gung-ho, very committed, upbeat'.[6] Companies value the person who is 'on the bus', not the one who dissents and challenges core values. Sinclair's MBA students often ask for a list to help them be good leaders; most don't want to stop to critique the management paradigm. They are seeking a leadership model. In this, they are very different from that subset, the cultural creatives, so keen to experiment and find new ways of operating. And a far cry too from the Generation Nexters who seek out difference as they enter the workforce. And we fear this group is pretty representative of prevailing attitudes in business. Leadership is a buzzword but the corporate world can often be afraid of digging too deeply into what it really means.

After many years as a high-achiever and successful academic, administrator and writer, Sinclair says, 'Workplaces to me have become highly inhibitive and a whole lot of things have helped that – the long hours, the technology. They have reinforced the idea that there is one persona that is more allowable than others. My view is that the self I wheel out at work is a very, very partial self. This raises the question of whether there is an authentic self trapped at home in the cupboard. While I don't think that it's that simple, we are increasingly expected to deliver a very particular performance in the workplace. Companies recruit for breadth of values and experience but make it progressively difficult to maintain that breadth.'[7]

That sense of a partial self drove Sinclair on a personal journey of discovery. When we first spoke to her it was early in 2003 and she had just begun a year of leave from the MBS – an effort to discover life beyond her admitted workaholism. She was just a couple of months into her 'idling' and was beginning to realise how much her sense of self was based on success at work. And she'd thought a lot about how much she'd had to bend in order to 'pass' in the system. 'Reflecting back, I realised I felt under a lot of pressure to be a person I wasn't completely comfortable with. I'm determined not to get into that space again.'[8] Now, after that year out, Sinclair is back at the Melbourne Business School but keen to bring some of the personal lessons around ego and energy back into her workplace.

It will be an interesting challenge because workplaces have always required people to fit in, to merge with the environment of the office, factory or restaurant. Real difference in the workplace challenges the discipline which keeps the system ticking over. But some of the traits considered desirable have changed over recent years. In *The Future of Success* Robert Reich argues that whereas in the old economy you did well by being well liked, by adopting an 'other directed personality', now you get ahead by being well marketed.[9] This is something people reared on an individualistic approach to their work take for granted. Skills are important, but the worker is a package, with points to be highlighted or disguised. Workers, especially in the knowledge and service sector, talk of selling themselves to the boss, of making the right pitch. When the pitch is rewarded it reinforces an acceptable way of being.

Over and over we see workers, in particular young women, consciously creating an image for the workplace. Their passion for work goes far beyond acquiring skills to a willingness to mould their identity. Competition for attention is fierce and Generations X and Next know this better than any other. The celebrity culture and the instant fame seen in reality television shows like *Big Brother* or *The Block* make younger people extremely savvy about carving out a persona that will be noticed. Many are astute marketers of themselves. It is hard to escape the feeling that in some way, we are all faking it.

Henry Ford wanted his workers to leave their brains at the gate and their personalities at home but today they are urged to bring both to the desk. Corporations ask employees to contribute ideas for new products and services. Some hire consultants to help stimulate an innovation culture. Emotional Intelligence, the idea of tapping the intuitive as well as the rational parts of the brain, is pushed as a positive. Dull and boring but reliable, once the perfect mix for many bureaucratised workplaces, is now nowhere near the right repertoire.

Yet the organisation that now asks you to bring your hearts and minds to work still looks for an acceptable 'you' and in our reporting we have seen little evidence that companies truly want you to be the same at work as you are at home or at the beach. They want employees to be authentic, but not too authentic. Even the contemporary debate about work/life balance reinforces the idea that we are different at work, that there is a dividing line between the two.

For Penny Dobson, the head of health care strategy and corporate affairs at Merck Sharp Dohme in Australia and a twenty-year veteran of the company, it's clear that the corporation needs to have workers whose values are aligned with the company's: 'Merck pays me a rent, they are renting a certain set of behaviours, and if

I don't deliver the behaviours, I don't get the rent. It's all about choices.'[10]

Those choices mean that workers will adopt various approaches to a 'viable personality' but there is little doubt that you do need one. One of the areas where we have seen a real shift in our own working lives is the extent to which challenge and dissent are discouraged – despite the rhetoric about the value of creative thinking people to your organisation. Once again there's a paradox here. Companies want creativity, but creativity that is *manageable* and ultimately non-threatening. They want workers to speak up, but only about some subjects. Truly original thinkers can find themselves as out of place in the modern office as they ever have. We sometimes hear a boss say that he or she does not want to employ clones of themselves because this will do nothing for their business. Sometimes they follow through. But once again the range of difference can be relatively narrow. The truth of organisations is that they accommodate difference only up to a point. In a high-pressure company, the 'viable personalities' are those that fit in and need little maintenance.

You might have been gobsmacked the first time your manager told you to bring him solutions, not problems, but it's a common phrase in big companies. It's an interesting twist to the idea that workers should be empowered. In this case, empowered to solve their own problems without any engagement from the bosses. In such an environment, there is little space for dissent. Asking questions and presenting problems can be a career-threatening move. A suggestion about how to improve the process may be welcomed, and held up as creative or innovative, but challenge can be dangerous. Just ask a CEO if they tolerate mistakes. If they are honest the answer is invariably no. All this tends to curb personality and flatten the culture of workplaces.

People are often watchful at work, mindful of not really saying what they think or reacting as they wish. This caution is not restricted to junior employees – in the end, everyone answers to someone and often managers survive on their ability to read the play. They step back and hold back. This is often the case for men. As female journalists, we've seen first-hand the extraordinary ability of male colleagues to hold their counsel and then feed back to the boss, the alpha male, what he already knows, even what he has already said. There's safety in waiting and men have centuries of conditioning to contend with here – they have often had to beware the powerful male who could take them on in a physical contest. Staying within clear parameters in the workplace comes far more naturally to many men than to most women. That said, women are often depicted as cautious at work and their own worst enemies in failing to speak out about what they think. Women can be naïve about the power of a good idea (no matter who came up with it) to sway the boss, while men can often be more political and realistic about merit.

Both men and women feel the restrictions of the workplace but for women, the denial of sexuality in the workplace can be especially tough. In Amanda Sinclair's 1998 book *Doing Leadership Differently* she argues that a model of leadership based on tough, heterosexual males means that women, and female sexuality, are largely excluded from the frame. While the overt alpha male sexuality defines corporate culture, setting the bar, as it were, for behaviour, women must deny a key part of their personalities at work. They must camouflage and blend. Sinclair does not suggest trying to take male sexuality out of the workplace but rather recognising that sexuality is part of us all and that it allows men and women to be more themselves, more complete, at work.[11] What is needed is the permission for different styles of being at work. This is far more than a debate about whether or not women are discriminated against at work in overt or covert ways. But the reality is that, especially for women, the tension involved in maintaining a certain workplace demeanour can be exhausting and take energy away from actually doing a good job.

There are efforts in popular culture to expand the repertoire. In the movie *Legally Blonde* the heroine is not exactly sexy, but she's certainly perky, as well as being a Harvard Law School graduate. She's a world away from the values of Harvard and the legal establishment and has to battle hard to retain her authentic self. In the end, she wins by drawing on the elements of her personality, like intuition, that are traditionally seen as female. Her successful defence of a client charged with murder rests on her knowledge of human nature and female behaviour. Another female character who stretches the boundaries is Erin Brokovich, as played by Julia Roberts in the eponymous film. In this case Brokovich is based on a real person, but the screen character is decidedly sexy and challenging at all levels. She wins against the system because she's a gutsy, real woman, not in spite of those characteristics.

Still, it's hard to believe the business world will absorb these Hollywood ideas quickly. Novelist Kate Jennings, who spent seven years working on Wall Street in the 1990s, has written a lot about the brutality of the financial world. 'It is', she says, 'very primitive, irrational and crude. It's also a culture that iconises gutsy men, rather than gutsy women.'[12] Jennings, an Australian who has lived in the United States for many years, had to swallow hard to keep going when she worked on the Street to support an ailing husband, a story she tells in her novel *Moral Hazard*.

In such a competitive work environment, there is little scope for playing with a range of identities. And not much opportunity to quarantine your private life. Once the system rewarded those who stuck at the job, even if they were not the best and brightest. Now, as Meaghan Morris says, workers are required to be 'one hundred per cent employee' and success is about the level of energy, mental strength and sheer testosterone (now found as much in women as men) a person applies to the job. It's about the 'quality of your desire' to grab the opportunities and put in the effort.[13] It's the kind of desire that can indeed be a substitute for sex. There's a sense in many companies that employees are required to be good ambassadors for the corporation as well as being effective workers. Workers are cautious about how they behave. Even the executive who runs the selection interviews for new positions is likely to take care with his or her behaviour. There's always the chance that a candidate will bad-mouth you outside the firm and damage you as well as the company.

Über-CEO Jack Welch says that if you want to win as a boss you have to *care* more than the next person. Work has to matter terribly to you if you want to win in today's environment: it has to matter more than family, sex and other relationships. The kind of balanced identity that some of those in his son's generation might seek is fine, getting home in time to see the kids, for example, but don't expect to be CEO if you choose that path. 'You can get a good job and you can have a fulfilled life and you can have flexi-time, but in the end if you want to run the company, or the division, it takes huge commitment and if you don't get a kick out of it, don't do it.'[14] It can be a powerful, heady trip and Welch should know. Welch expresses no regrets at the choices he has made. In an interview with *AFR BOSS* in 2003, he was feisty and uncompromising about the virtues of capitalism and a style of corporate behaviour that takes no prisoners.

Yet it seems to us that the 'winning at all costs' persona can be dangerous for companies. Obsessives might make successful CEOs but in other layers of management they are often so hard to work alongside that they just make everyone leave. There is more than one speed and downtime, on the job or off, is good for people.

The intense desire to succeed, which seems a prerequisite of getting the top jobs in today's competitive climate, is spread through the population unevenly, so much so that those who don't have it don't get a look in and often wind up being excluded from the economy, or at least the elite layers of the economy. It is the 'fittest' who survive at work. Take a straw poll of workers and you will find a range of reasons why people work at various degrees of intensity. Not everyone has the same drive. But today's system does not account for that shading. Says Meaghan Morris, 'There were lots of scathing references about time servers in the old system but at least it wasn't arbitrary. People knew the rules and while it may not have been fair, it was at least socially rational.'[15]

That approach was not always fair to individuals who were blocked from promotion by time-serving colleagues. And it is certainly not the driving force of markets interested in winners. Today's workers operate in a climate where there is intense competition for the interesting knowledge jobs in the economy. They fight it out in an environment where they are encouraged to use any competitive advantage they have. It's a world where employees are no longer shy about using their contacts to get their foot in the door, and a world where nepotism is no longer a dirty word. 'Whatever it takes' is the dominant creed in our private, public and working lives. Holding out for principle will not get you far in many organisations, no matter how many books you read about the importance of values.

Yet even if you win, you are likely to be a 'provisional winner'.[16] Winners must be constantly poised for the next battle, positioning themselves for the next job, reinventing themselves constantly just to keep ahead. As soon as they win, it's ground zero again for the next competition. There is no time for reflection, no time to pause. There's an adage in journalism that you are only as good as your last story. Now it's the same outside the newsroom. At one level, the competition is exciting, but not everyone is driven to constant reinvention.

The sense of a conforming culture in the work zone which rewards certain types of behaviour runs parallel with the post-modernist belief that we construct our own identities. There's also a strong rhetoric of choice. We talk about multi-tasking, multiple skills, diversity and reinvention at work. Meaghan Morris says that such ideas were launched into mainstream thinking at the moment when Australia, under a Labor government in the 1980s, began to deregulate away from fixed jobs, fixed expectations and fixed notions of work and identity. It was the end of regulated operations and the start of a more fluid approach in every area. Just as workers were being told that there were no fixed jobs any longer, no jobs that you could rely on forever, they were also being told that nothing much else was fixed either. As workers, they had to accept that they had multiple tasks, as people they had to understand there were multiple realities.

At the same time our work relationships have become instru-mental. Now that people are marked on their outcomes there is less sharing with colleagues. Relationships are seen in terms of what people can do for you – networking is very different from having a long lunch at the downtown Greek restaurant with the rest of the office. Once we would have been ashamed to contact a colleague after a gap of five or ten years to ask for a reference or a contact or a favour. You felt like a user to be so blatant about why you were getting in contact. That sense of propriety now seems almost old-fashioned in a world where workers make very precise and rapid calculations about the value of a professional contact or relationship. As journalists we have often been abashed at the extent to which we get up close and personal with subjects, then discard them once the story is written. Now we see a similar pattern emerging across other professions.

Such transactional behaviour does not come out of nowhere but rather stems from a performance-based work culture. When every exchange can be measured, it's scarcely surprising that workers want a result from every encounter. If the workplace asks you to constantly map your goals, regularly checks to see whether you have achieved them and rewards you when you do, you will take that approach into every part of your professional life. And if there is no real room at work for open-ended discussion and serendipity, surely that influences our behaviour outside work as well as at the office? Our professional and personal worlds merge, not just because we check our email at home or because we are constantly in mobile phone contact. They merge in deeper ways in terms of how we operate and think.

Once again, it is important to acknowledge this has long been the case, *The Organization Man* being the classic example. But it has become more pronounced because of the time we spend focused on work and the central role it plays in our lives. At least Organisation Man had a hinterland – the golf club, the martinis, the wife at home. In part that hinterland was due to the position of women in society. Middle-class women in particular stayed at home in the decades after the Second World War and were, in effect, given the role of custodian of non-work life. Men left the workplace to travel to a very different environment, one that was often restrictive for both partners but very different from the office. When it worked, the home provided an alternative to the speed and stress of a busy office. But there were other economic factors that allowed workers to quarantine aspects of their lives. Lack of competition and protected economies, unthreatened by the cheap labour and volatile capital which developed with global deregulation: all this meant a quieter life for many employees. It's a shock to pick up a novel like *Revolutionary Road*, written in 1952 by Richard Yates, and read about Organisation Man throwing back several martinis at lunch with colleagues. Today's workers know that long lunches are long gone and even a couple of drinks at lunchtime is a no-no if you want to survive. You can't afford to indulge when jobs are so competitive. And the chance of a hinterland is less now that women also work and much of family life takes place to strict timetables. The end result is that work, and the personality that we create for work, tends to dominate.

Consultant Viv Read believes the organisation is increasingly mediocre in its outlook and the way work is organised. She looks back over several years of working with organisations and sees less interest now in how we can make life better for workers.[17] And doesn't a bland work persona lead to a mediocre society? If companies measure success by having compliant employees who share their views, will employees be imaginative in the way they go about their work? How do you keep the workforce fresh and invigorated when you want them to fit into a relatively narrow template of behaviour?

We have talked in earlier chapters about the heavy demands corporations make on employees in terms of time on the job. Again, it's not all bad. You don't have to be a workaholic to sometimes find solace at the office. For many people, it's the one space in their lives that they can really control. Families and intimate relationships are often messy exercises and work is an attractive option. At work, you find order. Long hours can also reinforce your sense of self and your worth. Many of us judge our work in a market-driven system by how much we earn, but staying late bolsters importance and encourages us to think we are central to the functioning of the office. And it can help justify why we are earning more when we can't show any physical output that differentiates us from a more junior worker. If you give up evenings and weekends you are demonstrating to yourself and others that you are worth the pay.

Nancy Milne remembers a time in the 1970s when, working

for a small law firm, 'everyone used to lay down tools at 5.30 p.m. and go to the boardroom for drinks, every day'. It was a bit of an anachronism but not that unusual. It was the 1980s when people started working longer and longer hours. The hours in law firms are now legendary. 'It's nothing for our guys in M & A [mergers and acquisitions] to stay all through the night . . . there are people wandering around on a Saturday night at 11 o'clock trying to finalise a document, and they have not slept for four or five days.'[18]

Is all this really necessary? Sometimes, yes, but often we hang on to a long hours culture because to resist it sends a message to others that we don't care enough. For professionals, email has had a big impact. Meaghan Morris, on leave, gets up early to write but first switches on for her emails. Once at that time, just before dawn, she would have walked the dog and had time to think. Now she handles her emails. The job never stops and the test in the twenty-first century is who will choose to switch on and who will choose to switch off. Switch off and you are not dedicated and eventually not on top of your brief. The message is clear. If you want to win, never turn off. This wide acceptance of the acceptable personality has been internalised by a generation hooked on work. To be professional is to be consumed by work and follow those internal rules which are potentially far more powerful than any external pressures. In Japan, salary men vie to leave the office last, to indicate that they are committed. But it's not just hours in the office that force changes to our personalities. It's the single-mindedness that is demanded of us as workers that can crowd out other ways of thinking and being.

One of the things that bothers Amanda Sinclair is the extent to which our debates about work never question the central paradigms but entrench the system. She argues that our work/life balance debate of recent years has been based not around asking if we should work these long hours, work full-time rather than part-time, but around who should pay for childcare. It is a debate that entrenches the system, assumes that work is the most powerful motivator and that good work is the most powerful index of success. But if you narrow the discussion to who pays, rather than to whether shorter hours or better structured part-time work is possible, you sell workers short.

Her professional research into the narrow ways in which work, success and leadership have been defined in our culture has set Sinclair thinking about how any of this can be changed. Are we naïve to think that we can make organisations operate differently? 'Perhaps while institutional structures are so resistant to change, the path to innovation may lie in individuals making radical changes,' she says. 'Maybe we need to get subsets within organisations operating in different ways, maybe we see small cells emerging where people can work differently, have different connections to their jobs.'[19] In her analysis of leaders, Sinclair looks for people who do it differently, who have more 'shading', more layers, and are at least reflective about the process and the system within which we work. We need critics as well as cheerleaders in our organisations.

Our own investigations into work, and particularly the way work takes place within big organisations, has convinced us that now is the time to begin playing with some options. Without sentimentalising the past, we need to have a broader conversation about what really constitutes a viable personality for today's workplace. Jack Welch may well be right when he says that you'll have a different life if you don't make it to the top rung. But Welch's go-getter persona is surely not the only available path to success.

At the other end of the spectrum sit commentators who are very distressed at the creation of 'economic man'. It's almost old-fashioned to talk about 'quality of life' these days, but Charles Birch, one of Australia's internationally renowned biologists and economists, uses the term happily. 'Do many corporates care about quality of life?' he asked one of us in late 2003 as he prepared for the launch of his new book, *Life and Work: Challenging Economic Man*, co-authored with management lecturer David Paul.[20] It's a hard question to answer. There's such a gulf between what Birch and the CEO of a multinational define as 'quality of life' for employees.

Books like *Life and Work* challenge the assumptions that corporates must get employees to work harder and harder to make bigger profits. Birch and Paul suggest that if corporations could only get their relationships with workers sorted, profits would follow. They urge companies to treat their workers with more dignity and to recognise their spiritual needs. Such language has long seemed out of place at work where employees and unions have struggled for physical and financial fairness but tended to leave the spiritual out of the equation.

We've begun to feel that some commentators want to turn the company and organisation into the church that is fading and the family that is under threat. Richard Barrett, a Colorado-based former civil engineer who worked for the World Bank before he reinvented himself in the 1990s as an organisational consultant, talks of the 'seven levels of consciousness' in workers and organisations. Meeting Barrett at the Menzies Hotel in central Sydney in late 2003, he says that when he walks into the world's boardrooms and starts talking about consciousness he gets a great reception. Boards and CEOs 'get it' immediately. These days, he can even use a word like 'soul' without causing a riot among the executives. Barrett says business attracts some of the most innovative and creative people around, who are inspired to do well, achieve and build wealth. But when the basic needs are filled they start looking for more. In a sense, they are trying to discover their true identities.

'There is a general shift in consciousness going on in the Western world,' he says, and organisations have to respond. Barrett says organisations will move, in the next few years, to a new approach towards making decisions. Rather than looking backwards and trying to see the past and focus on what they 'believe', they will start looking forward to see what sort of values they want to have in their organisations. What do they want to experience? What do they want their people to experience? 'The old paradigm [of work] was fear-driven but we have had enough of fear-driven,' Barrett argues.[21]

When we look across the workforce today, we see companies keen to have perfect workers on their payrolls, with that perfection often defined in terms of behaviour, rather than skills. For their part, workers seem very aware of the need to package their identities in ways that suit the boss, so much so that the viable work personality often overshadows the way they present outside work. In other words, work wins. We've been amazed at times at the growing homogeneity of work personalities. Once it was the dress-for-success suits which made everyone feel the same; now they're as likely to share a demeanour as a fashion brand. And there's a sense too that work relationships are transactional, an approach which also influences personality and behaviour at work. This 'nothing for nothing' culture links neatly with a 'win at all costs' approach which is implicit in the statements of leaders like Jack Welch. But it raises a significant concern about the power of this framework to shape the world beyond work and our society.

1. Bayne, Martha. 'Charles the Excellent', *The Baffler*, Vol. 1, Number 15, pp. 59–63.
2. Interview with Meaghan Morris.
3. Cited in Deeble, Sandra. Article in 'My Career' section of *The Sydney Morning Herald*, 28 September, 2001. Reprinted from *The Guardian*.
4. Interview with Carl Rhodes.

5. Onsman, Harry. *Management Powertools*. McGraw-Hill, 2003, p. 242.
6. Interview with Amanda Sinclair.
7. Ibid.
8. Ibid.
9. Reich, op cit., p. 154. Reich refers to work by sociologist, David Riesman. The 'other directed personality' seeks 'above all else to be approved by his peers,' Reich writes.
10. Interview with Penny Dobson.
11. Sinclair, Amanda. *Doing Leadership Differently: Gender, Power and Sexuality in a Changing Business Culture*. Melbourne University Press, 1998.
12. Jennings, op cit.
13. Interview with Meaghan Morris.
14. Jack Welch made these comments during a presentation at a lunch in Sydney in 2003.
15. Interview with Meaghan Morris.
16. Ibid.
17. Interview with Viv Read.
18. Interview with Nancy Milne.
19. Interview with Amanda Sinclair.
20. Interview with Charles Birch.
21. Trinca, Helen. 'Corporate consciousness stripped bare', *The Australian Financial Review*, 27 January 2004, p. 42.

Conclusion

IN OUR INTRODUCTION WE EXPLAINED our credentials for writing a book about work. The nature of what we do as journalists writing for and editing a magazine about work means that every day in the office we are reviewing the latest thinking on this subject. From reading the latest academic research to analysing the latest management trend. We've watched the *Who Moved My Cheese?* phenomenon and interviewed Tom Peters. Talked to Edward de Bono about his latest creativity theory, got on the phone to Daniel Goleman in New York to talk emotional intelligence and listened to Michael Porter in an auditorium filled with hundreds of smartly dressed executives. From time to time we've visited business schools and sat in on executive workshops, and even completed a battery of psychometric tests in the name of research. We have trawled through compendiums of management theory to find who came up with the Peter Principle or coined the term 're-engineering'. We've visited the offices of CEOs from

Westpac to BHP and David Jones. Heard writer Anne Summers and Woolworths director Di Grady talk about gender and work. The theories, the books and the ideas keep coming in. The flow has just got faster and faster.

During this process we still believed there was something that wasn't being tackled. There's an enormous amount of literature on every nuance of jobs, management and efficiency. But so much of what we have seen doesn't really come to grips with how we feel about work – the way we think about it and what that means for the future.

It's not straightforward. If there's one thing that has been reinforced for us it's that our relationship with work is more complex than ever. The writing of this book and our own experience as workers have left us with a heightened sense of the contradictions about this part of our lives. The need to find simple solutions accelerates in response to this messy reality. That's why so many of these management gimmicks get so much attention. Many of us crave an easy answer to why we behave the way we do at work.

It's such a central part of our lives that taking stock of our relationship with our jobs is more important than ever. This is not a one-dimensional task, of course, or something that has potential to be resolved. The relationship most twenty-first-century employees have with their jobs is constantly changing. It is more complicated than ever, as a direct result of the emphasis we now put on the world of work. And our attempts to reflect on this relationship are lagging well behind the sophisticated reality.

When we started out in the workforce there was an understanding that you owed something to your employer. You were part of their domain and stuck with the rules. Now many of us are in a new transactional workspace, where there's always an outcome and every opportunity can be turned to your advantage. Once networking was about socialising and the results were intangible. Today you've failed unless you've pocketed a business card. In Australia most of us don't work in manufacturing or traditional industries any more. We are more likely to be behind a counter, in a professional firm or a call centre. The service sector is taking over in more than just a physical sense and is having an impact on how we think.

When we started to read about emotional labour and the workplace it really resonated with us. The call to bring yourself lock, stock and barrel to work filters through the many corporate efforts to control behaviour and culture. It doesn't have to be this way.

The work transaction has changed dramatically. In the past it centred on the weekly pay packet – you worked, they paid, the rules were usually clear and the hierarchy was in place. There was security but little room for negotiation. Today the wage contract is just the start of the elaborate negotiations that define the way we operate at work. Today's workers increasingly negotiate their own way at work. For each task a return is expected. What's in it for me? Why should I come on board? What can you give me to keep me here?

This shouldn't surprise. The props keeping people at work, loyal and unquestioning, have been pulled apart. The career in a traditional form no longer exists. Permanent jobs last as long as the economic cycle permits. Corporations no longer feel they owe employees anything and workers understand that. In just a decade or so workers have made the transition from seeing work as a binding contract to a series of transactions. These transactions extend over the whole of our lives. Every realm is touched by work. So many of the traditional mediators of meaning – the church, the family, politics – are straining at the edges and being supplanted by the market.

The obsession with work is increasing. Our expectations about what work can deliver are much more weighty than a decade or two ago. Work sits at the centre of our lives and we respond strongly to the demands of employers to commit to their goals. But within that deal, employees are beginning to realise that they are not passive players. They sense they have leverage, not to change the macro-structures of business, but to negotiate a way through it. The executive who steps back to a less intense job before moving ahead two years down the track is engaging in the kind of zigzag career that was once seen as the road to nowhere. Today, it's a viable option, for some at least. The executives who choose this path are not rejecting the modern work ethic. They are as reliant on work for personal meaning as anyone. But they are using a new understanding of work which challenges the expectation that there is only one way to operate.

This potential to negotiate a more individual track through company and career has been helped by the emergence of a highly educated workforce which, for the first time, includes significant numbers of women. That's a change that should not be underestimated. This impact has been described to us as the 'hairdryer in the hotel room' phenomenon. When the majority of the workforce was male, there was no demand from business travellers for facilities such as a hairdryer to be supplied in hotel rooms. Now they are routinely provided and everyone benefits. It's a small example of a much broader trend. Women workers are bringing about change in the way everyone works, albeit slowly, and, it is to be hoped, they are altering the idea of what is an acceptable or successful career.

The impact of women on the structure of work has largely gone unnoticed in much of the popular writing about the workplace. When it is addressed, the debate focuses on whether or not women are breaking through the glass ceiling. That's important but more significant is the way the presence of women, who are also primary carers, is shifting expectations about the way work should be organised on a practical basis. Look at what is happening with flexible hours of work and parental or caring leave. It's no longer necessary to lie about attending a school concert. It's a small step but our sense is there will be more battles won, including the demand for permanent part-time careers. It is very early days but slowly attitudes are changing. Gradually, employees of both sexes are seeing alternatives to the monolithic, full-time career path. They certainly question the equation that long hours equals productivity equals career success. They will remain committed to work but will question the notion that the only way to measure commitment is through hours at the desk.

Some aspects of our working lives are better – for some of us there is more control. And most of us are smarter about what goes on around us. Increasingly aware of the many organisational attempts to pull them into line, employees from a range of jobs and businesses are analysing the workplace and working out just what is acceptable for them and where the organisation is crossing a line. The frustration with corporate language and management-speak reflects this concern.

Far from being powerless, a new generation will enter jobs with the expectation that they have the right to negotiate and question their employer. These transactional workers will see themselves as equal partners in a way that goes further than the sort of partnership promised by corporates in the 1990s. That decade's corporate spin around empowerment was, in large measure, a management exercise designed to boost productivity. The empowerment was entirely the gift of the employer and was heavily constrained. But the idea of individual power within the workplace took hold. This time around, young workers will bring a certain set of skills or abilities to the transaction but they expect immediate results. And such a proactive approach is not confined to Generation X. Even Baby Boomers are reassessing their relationship with the organisation, partly because there are few alternatives for employment for most of us. And these people have seen the process of performance management, where everything you do on the job is measured. This has reinforced the transaction mentality.

It's not all a bleak push and pull, however. Sometimes the transactional nature of work means there's more clarity about roles and responsibilities and can make the expectations we have of work more realistic. It can mean jobs are more satisfying. On the other hand, corporate attempts to get employees pulling in the same direction and working harder are often presented dishonestly. Our gripe with culture programs and measurement is that while they have the potential to put the emphasis on people and their value to a business, too often they are actually concerned with productivity. A more direct approach would save money and treat employees with more respect. Their antennae for corporate lip service are very sensitive and should be respected. Presenteeism is one symptom of a workplace where the stress and frustration of too much corporate manipulation triggers a cut-off by workers.

At every level in organisations today, we are seeing employees keen to recast the work contract. We know for many people work sits somewhere between sheer drudgery and fulfilment, but across the spectrum there are opportunities for change. Of course many will continue to do a good job and collect the pay packet, accepting the rules of the boss. But we think an increasing number will want more.

We don't exaggerate the power of individual workers to change the way work is organised. Most of us still turn up at regular times, in big organisations, spend long hours at the job and take some direction from the boss. But we are becoming more educated and more educated about work. The writing of this book has been a liberating process because of the very central role work plays in our own lives. Even though our jobs involve much thinking about the themes of this book, the opportunity to bring the strands together and analyse what is happening has been intellectually satisfying and revealing.

The effort by companies to colonise us and encourage us to live and breathe the mission statement has triggered a backlash. Workers have been forced to examine the culture of work and in doing so they have become far more aware of how they can be manipulated. It's been the basis for a more proactive worker.

In many ways this new equation means our investment in work may intensify. We started this book to examine our love affair with work and the idea that it competes with fundamental human desires around sex and social contact. It is clear to us now that this preoccupation with seeking identity through work will not diminish. Once that identity depended, in part, on the organisation. That's far less likely today even though the organisation is as strong as ever. Now even permanent employees may see themselves as individual portfolio workers. Identity is tied to your work, not your company.

But the company effort to win our hearts and align our values with its own were not wasted. Since the 1990s the wave of corporate change programs and mission statements has shifted the language of work. Employees have absorbed the corporate and market values almost subconsciously. This is not only because of the demise of unions but flows from the maturity of the market economy and its infiltration into every corner of life.

Many of us are more literate about the process but are still not free agents when it comes to work. Capitalism has indeed colonised much of the space for an alternative debate about meaning. Nothing we have learnt in the process of writing this book suggests that will change.

What, then, of the future?

A few years ago it was not cool to be enthusiastic about work.

Jobs were boring and repetitive and part of the establishment. During the 1980s, work was necessary but still a means to an end. A good job was desirable but it was distinctly unfashionable to tie your identity to work. By the 1990s the world had changed and work was not only cool, it was the way many of us built our identity. The market was God and work moved to centre stage. By the time the century ended and the dot com collapse dampened our enthusiasm for technology stocks, the landscape had changed so profoundly it was hard sometimes to see how far we had come. From clerical workers to consultants and call centre staff, we are our jobs. We expect much from them and, as the devastation after redundancy shows, the impact of withdrawal from a job is severe. The repercussions of our reliance on work for meaning are diffuse and profound.

Our research shows us that work will be a rich area of meaning for many people. Both employers and employees will continue to wrestle with how this plays out. For a start, don't expect the corporate quest to get inside the workers' souls to falter. If volunteer mode is a corny way to talk about company indoctrination then be assured it will be replaced with others. There's too much to be gained from convincing workers to get on board. An increasingly sophisticated workforce will make such pursuit essential.

At the same time the assumption that the job will deliver meaning will encourage workers to keep investing their time and energy. We see the workplace becoming a viable alternative to the other parts of the community. Already workers gain social satisfaction from their interactions with colleagues, spending as much time with them as close friends or family. More and more the work group, often a sub-unit within a department, will take on the role of the family and friends network for many people. In this way, meaning will not just rely on reaching targets or getting contracts for the organisation, but on a more complex set of relationships and social alliances. The sub-unit could be the place where many of us find a way to moderate the impact of the organisation, where we experiment with new models.

This is where work patterns and hours on duty could be renegotiated. It is perhaps an arena where managers will find some solutions to the demands of workers for more flexibility and alternatives to full-time jobs. One of the most critical of these for society is the problem of how workers can also be parents. If capitalism continues to demand high levels of engagement and productivity it seems likely more and more people will find themselves without children. The question of balancing work and family is not just about a rethink of childcare but of priorities as an advanced society. Options worth further investigation include developing a more structured approach to time out of the career and viable alternatives to the full-time job.

There's a bigger issue at play here. Will there be time left for relationships of any sort, let alone those involving life partners and reproduction? The juggernaut of the market makes enormous demands on time and energy. Without some tempering of this trend, it seems entirely possible that we will simply narrow our sense of what it means to be successful. Children and relationships could be a luxury many people find they simply can't afford.

When we began our working lives and for many years after that, we believed that work could be controlled, that if we worked long and hard, we could tie up the ends and cross the t's. We saw our jobs as beasts to be tamed and ourselves as people we had to bring into line to perform successfully. If we failed to do this, if the untidy elements of organisations or roles persisted, it meant we were neither smart nor resilient enough. Or maybe we were just not spending enough time in the office. It's taken a while, but we've come to understand that work, like human behaviour, can often be unpredictable, uncontainable and unmeasurable. Our work has given us a new understanding: that work is not control-lable in the way that the system would have us believe, but that equally, we are not powerless against that unpredictability. Nor are we powerless against the organisation and the avalanche of cultural change programs or inspirational texts or the countless other methods that a company uses to turn us into the kind of workers they think they need for the twenty-first century. In the end, the sheer unpredictability of humans is what gives business its energy.

Ultimately, work is about messy realities, not finely tuned blueprints. Despite the technology, it remains incredibly human. Modern managers love to talk about the intangible elements of the workplace and how they determine the value of organisations in a knowledge economy. But they rarely factor in the intangibles like fear and greed or even just the pleasure of working with a particu-lar person and the satisfaction of finishing off a project. But workers know these intangibles. They take for granted that work is nowhere as logical and rational as the textbooks would have us believe. They know that being at work is intensely complex and potentially life-changing. And sometimes, just sometimes, it is indeed better than sex.

Bibliography

Aldridge, Alan. *Consumption*. Cambridge: Polity, 2003.

Andresky Fraser, Jill. *White Collar Sweatshop: The Deterioration of Work and its Rewards in Corporate America*. New York: W.W. Norton & Company, 2001.

Bauman, Zygmunt. *Liquid Love*. Cambridge: Polity, 2003.

Beder, Sharon. *Global Spin: The Corporate Assault on Environmentalism*. Carlton, Victoria: Scribe Publications.

Beder, Sharon. *Selling the Work Ethic: From Puritan Pulpit to Corporate PR*. Carlton, Victoria: Scribe Publications, 2000.

Birch, Charles and Paul, David. *Life and Work: Challenging Economic Man*. Sydney: University of New South Wales Press, 2003.

Blake, Darryl. *Skroo the Rules! What the World's Most Productive Workplace Does Differently*. Melbourne: Information Australia, 2001.

Bronson, Po. *What Should I Do With My Life?*. New York: Random House, 2002.

Ciulla, Joanne B. *The Working Life: The Promise and Betrayal of Modern Work*. New York: Three Rivers Press, 2001.

Davenport, Thomas H. and Beck, John C. *The Attention Economy: Understanding the New Currency of Business*. Cambridge, MA: Harvard Business School Press, 2001.

DeMarco, Tom. *Slack: Getting Past Burnout, Busywork and the Myth of Total Efficiency*. New York: Broadway Books, 2002.

Donkin, Richard. *Blood, Sweat and Tears: The Evolution of Work*. New York: Texere, 2001.

Drucker, Peter. *The Practice of Management*. New York: Harper & Row, 1955.

Florida, Richard. *The Rise of the Creative Class: And How It's Transforming Work, Leisure, Community and Everyday Life*. New York: Basic Books, 2002.

Frank, Thomas. *One Market Under God: Extreme Capitalism, Market Populism and the End of Economic Democracy*. New York: Vintage, 2001.

Gini, Al. *My Job, My Self: Work and the Creation of the Modern Individual*. London: Routledge, 2001.

Goleman, Daniel. *Emotional Intelligence*. London: Bloomsbury, 1996.

Gordon, David M. *Fat and Mean: The Corporate Squeeze of Working Americans and the Myth of Managerial 'Downsizing'*. New York: Martin Kessler Books, 1996.

Gratton, Lynda. *Living Strategy: Putting People at the Heart of Corporate Purpose*. London: Financial Times Prentice Hall 2000.

Hamel, Gary. *Leading the Revolution*. Cambridge, MA: Harvard Business School Press, 2000.

Handy, Charles. *The Hungry Spirit*. London: Random House Business, 1998.

Hewlett, Sylvia Ann. *Baby Hunger: The New Battle for Motherhood*. New York: Atlantic Books, 2002.

Hochschild, Arlie Russell. *The Commercialization of Intimate Life: Notes from Home and Work*. Berkeley: University of California Press, 2003.

Houellebecq, Michel. *Platform*. London: William Heinemann, 1999.

Hutton, Will. *The State We're In*. London: Jonathan Cape, 1995.

Jennings, Kate. *Moral Hazard*. Sydney: Picador Australia, 2003.

Kleiner, Art. *Who Really Matters: The Core Group Theory of Power, Privilege and Success*. New York: Currency, 2003.

Lowenstein, Wendy. *Weevils at Work: What's Happening to Work in Australia – An Oral Record*. Annandale, NSW: Catalyst Press, 1997.

Mayo, Andrew. *The Human Value of the Enterprise*. London: Nicholas Brealey Publishing, 2001.

Morgan, Gareth. *Images of Organization*. Beverly Hills: Sage Publications, 1986.

Nördstrom, Kjell and Ridderstråle, Jonas. *Funky Business: Talent Makes Capital Dance*. London: Financial Times Prentice Hall, 1999.

Onsman, Harry. *Management Powertools*. North Ryde, NSW: McGraw Hill, 2003.

Palahniuk, Chuck. *Fight Club*. New York: W.W. Norton & Company, 1996.

Pearson, Allison. *I Don't Know How She Does It*. London: Chatto & Windus, 2002.

Perlman, Elliot. *Seven Types of Ambiguity*. Sydney: Picador Australia, 2003.

Pink, Daniel H. *Free Agent Nation: The Future of Working for Yourself*. New York: Warner Books, 2002.

Pocock, Barbara. *The Work/Life Collision*, Annandale, NSW: Federation Press, 2003.

Postrel, Virginia. *The Substance of Style: How the Rise of Aesthetic Value is Remaking Commerce, Culture, and Consciousness*. New York: HarperCollins, September 2003.

Ray, Paul and Anderson, Sherry Ruth. *The Cultural Creatives*. New York: Three Rivers Press, 2001.

Reich, Robert. *The Future of Success: Working and Living in the New Economy*. New York: Vintage, 2002.

Reichheld, Frederick F. *Loyalty Rules!: How Today's Leaders Build Lasting Relationships*. Cambridge, MA: Harvard Business School Press, 2001.

Schor, Juliet. *The Overworked American: The Unexpected Decline of Leisure*. New York: Basic Books, 1993.

Scott, Ted and Harker, Phil. *The Myth of Nine to Five: Work, Workplaces and Workplace Relationships*. North Sydney, NSW: Richmond Ventures, 2002.

Semler, Ricardo. *The Seven-Day Weekend*. London: Random House, 2003.

Senge, Peter. *The Fifth Discipline: The Art and Practice of the Learning Organisation*. New York: Currency, 1990.

Sinclair, Amanda. *Doing Leadership Differently: Gender, Power and Sexuality in a Changing Business Culture*. Melbourne: Melbourne University Press, 1998.

Summers, Anne, *The End of Equality*. Milsons Point, NSW: Random House Australia, 2003.

Terkel, Studs. *Working*. New York: The New Press, 1972.

Tingle, Laura. *Chasing the Future: Recession, Recovery and the New Politics in Australia*. Port Melbourne: Reed Books, 1994.

Watson, Don. *Death Sentence: The Decay of Public Language*. Milsons Point, NSW: Knopf Australia, 2003.

Whyte, William H. *Organization Man*. London: Jonathan Cape, 1956.

Yates, Richard. *Revolutionary Road*. New York: Vintage, 2000.

Zemke, Ron, et al. *Generations at Work: Managing the Clash of Veterans, Boomers, Xers, and Nexters in your Workplace*. New York: Amacom, 2000.

Permissions

For permission to cite in various ways, acknowledgement is made to the following:

Perseus Books Group, for excerpt from Richard Florida, *The Rise of the Creative Class*.

Polity Press, for excerpts from Zygmunt Bauman, *Liquid Love* and Alan Aldridge, *Consumption*.

Studs Terkel, for excerpt from *Working*.

University of Pennsylvania Press for excerpt from William H. Whyte, *The Organization Man*.

Random House Inc. for excerpt from Thomas Frank, *One Market Under God*.

Excerpt from *Seven Types of Ambiguity* by Elliot Perlman reprinted by permission of Pan Macmillan Australia Pty Ltd. © Elliot Perlman.

The European Management Journal for excerpt from Lynda Gratton and Sumantra Ghosal, 'Managing Personal Human Capital: A new ethos for the "volunteer" employee'.

The BBC for excerpt from *The Office* website.

The London Review of Books and Katha Pollitt for excerpt from 'In the family's way'.

Federation Press for excerpt from Barbara Pocock, *The Work/Life Collision*.

Acknowledgements

THANKS TO OUR COLLEAGUES PAST and present at *AFR BOSS* magazine for their energy and interest in the core subject of this book, and our editors and colleagues at the *Australian Financial Review*. The many conversations we've had over the years with these people have helped shape our approach to the subject and this book.

There are so many academics, writers, practitioners and workers who have shared their experiences and ideas with us that it's hard to thank them all individually. But special thanks to Dexter Dunphy, Viv Read, Amanda Sinclair, Bill Ford, Graeme Russell and Jane Caro. Many other people gave their time to be interviewed or to help us check details and we are grateful for their help.

Our friends and families stayed patient and interested over the two years we spent researching and writing this book. Their support was – as always – invaluable, and some of them even weighed in with ideas and read chapters.

Thanks especially to Patricia, Geraldine, Roger and Brendan Fox; David Koob, Simone, Evelyn and Antonia Fox Koob; Jo Trinca, Christopher, Robin, Tom, James and Alexander Ballantyne;

Jenny, Geoff and Maggie McPhee; Mathew Trinca, Robert Bolton, Bob Swift, Mathilde Swift-Nolen, Geraldine Doogue, Ian Carroll, Lyndall Crisp, Frannie and Garrett Jones, Hugh Lamberton, Julie Macken, Samantha Wright, Rosemary Johnston, Michele Jackson, Jane Ford, David Harman, Helen Connealy; and to Meredith Curnow, Jessica Dettmann and the team at Random House.

And finally, a thank you to our respective book clubs, where much robust discussion has taken place and to our many good friends who talked endlessly about work, listened to our theories and engaged so enthusiastically in the project. This book owes much to all of you.

March 2004